AN INTERCULTURAL WORSHIP HANDBOOK

AN INTERCULTURAL WORSHIP HANDBOOK

*Routes, Tools and Guideposts
for the Journey*

Ian Collinge

CANTERBURY
PRESS

© Ian Collinge 2025

First published in 2025 by the Canterbury Press Norwich

Editorial office
3rd Floor, Invicta House
110 Golden Lane,
London EC1Y 0TG, UK
www.canterburypress.co.uk

Canterbury Press is an imprint of Hymns Ancient & Modern Ltd
(a registered charity)

Hymns Ancient & Modern® is a registered trademark of
Hymns Ancient & Modern Ltd
13A Hellesdon Park Road, Norwich,
Norfolk NR6 5DR, UK

All rights reserved. No part of this publication may be reproduced,
stored in a retrieval system, or transmitted,
in any form or by any means, electronic, mechanical,
photocopying or otherwise, without the prior permission of
the publisher, Canterbury Press.

The Author has asserted his right under the Copyright, Designs and Patents Act 1988 to be
identified as the Author of this Work

Scripture quotations taken from the Holy Bible, New International Version, Anglicised edition.
Copyright © 1979, 1984, 2011 by Biblica, Inc. Used by permission.
All rights reserved worldwide.
And where indicated from the ESV Bible (The Holy Bible, English Standard Version),
copyright © 2001 by Crossway, a publishing ministry of Good News Publishers.
Used by permission. All rights reserved.

British Library Cataloguing in Publication data

A catalogue record for this book is available
from the British Library

ISBN: 978 1 78622 659 4

EU GPSR Authorised Representative
LOGOS EUROPE, 9 rue Nicolas Poussin, 17000, LA ROCHELLE, France
E-mail: Contact@logoseurope.eu

Typeset by Regent Typesetting

Contents

Foreword by Graham Kendrick	ix
Foreword by Joy and Jaewoo Kim	xi
Acknowledgements	xiii
List of Tools	xv
Introduction	xvii
1 Seeing: Vision and Motivations	1
2 Bones: Knowing Your Community	11
3 Listening: Where Intercultural Worship Starts	23
4 Dreaming: What It Could Bring About	32
5 Singing: Musical Diversity in Worship	55
6 Understanding: The Impact of Heart Music	72
7 Appreciating: Cultural Ways of Encountering God	90
8 Creating: Putting Flesh on the Bones	105
9 Rising: Improving and Developing	128
10 Integrating: A Culture of Many Cultures	143
Appendix A: Seven Top Tips	158
Appendix B: Wider Applications	161
References and Resources	168
Contacts	176

Dedicated to Helen
my wife
soul mate
passionate lover of Jesus
and
fellow traveller into worship
on earth as in heaven.

TO GOD ALONE BE THE GLORY

Foreword

Graham Kendrick

The first time I discovered that there was such a thing as an ethnodoxologist was at a gathering of songwriters. It came from the lips of Ian Collinge, who introduced himself as one. As he went on to explain what such a person did, and particularly when he began to unpack the term 'heart music', I sat up even straighter, recognizing a vital dynamic I knew about by experience but for which I didn't have a developed language, tools or signposts. On my travels I had for years been troubled by discovering how good and authentic expressions of praise and worship music emerging from one part of the world could drown out the sounds of local languages, styles and expressions in another. The irony was that my travel destinations were largely determined by where my own English-language songs had gone ahead of me in foreign translations. I often found myself prompted to say in effect: 'I am honoured that you are singing my songs in your language. I hope they have served you well, but I'd love it if you used them to "prime the pump" of your own creativity. You have something unique to offer God from your own culture and language, so may I encourage you to write your own songs.'

I had stumbled across just one example of why this book is needed. But I consider my challenge simple compared to what many leaders face today: negotiating the complexities of leading congregations of diverse languages and cultural identities under the same roof week after week. When once upon a time a fair degree of distinctive cultural identity – where people formed their 'heart music' rooted in physical geography and local community – might have been assumed, this is less and less the case as wars, climate issues and the like propel mass migration, and as digital connectivity heats up the cultural melting-pot. The need for clear thinking and wise action has become more pressing.

Around the time I was writing songs for an international outdoor event called the Global March for Jesus, the same scripture gripped us that is foundational to Ian's book: Revelation 7.9–10, describing an innumerable multitude from every nation, tribe, people and language worshipping with one voice. I remember seeing in my imagination the earth turning in space as worship rose to God from believers of every nation, people, tribe and language in every time zone. Their worship rose like multi-coloured threads, the different colours representing their unique gifts of worship, a beautiful variety of expressions. The threads rose and weaved in and out of each other, forming a gigantic banner arching over the globe. As the design took shape, I saw it was the face of Jesus. Had all the threads been monochrome, so would be the banner and so would be the face of Jesus. How desperately sad to be a monochrome church when the testimony to his grace and glory should be in vivid colours!

In this very practical book, Ian brings clear thinking and clear language to matters of cultural identity – a subject that has many pitfalls in speech and practice.

He has walked the walk, engaging with people of cultures and world views very different from his own, and offers many helpful examples and suggestions. He sets out 'Routes, Tools and Guideposts' to inspire the reader to press on with their own vision for culturally diverse worship. If you are gripped by such a vision, wrestling with the challenges of intercultural worship, or see that it may await you just around the corner, then this book will be an invaluable companion on the journey – a friend and mentor who has been this way before.

Graham Kendrick
Songwriter of over 450 songs, singer, worship leader, speaker
and one of the founders of March for Jesus

Foreword

Joy and Jaewoo Kim

Many years ago, during our own journey towards intercultural worship as Korean Americans living in the United States, we met Ian. His rich experiences interacting with people from diverse cultures worldwide, including his significant time spent in Asia, gave us the sense that he affirmed our own cultures but also saw us beyond our skin colour or our ethnicity. He knew how to ask insightful questions that stirred thoughts we had never considered. He consistently maintained the posture of a learner, even while teaching. In this book you will encounter Ian through his words, and we believe you will also connect with his character interwoven throughout his writing. Reading this book is like having a personal guide and companion, humbly and patiently walking alongside you on the journey of intercultural worship.

Now those who are beginning this journey have this guide that points them in the right direction based on biblical foundation. It is like a map designed by someone who has walked this path with an intention to guide and support the travellers. Ian's tone of voice in this book is kind and understanding. He recognizes not only the worth and beauty of this journey but also the challenges and difficulties, drawn from his own experiences of navigating many obstacles along the way. Readers at any stage of the journey – whether they are beginners grasping the basics, seasoned travellers reaffirming their vision or those who are wondering what's next in between – will find what follows encouraging and greatly helpful, as it was for us even before this book was born into the world.

AN INTERCULTURAL WORSHIP HANDBOOK

We wish it had been available 15 years ago when we were beginners. Our journey would have been significantly smoother, enriched by its wealth of insights and practical tools and guideposts, solidly based on extensive research in the field of intercultural worship. However, we trust God's timing and are excited that this guide is now available to help readers worldwide understand the vision of intercultural worship and equip them to embody it humbly and skilfully. We have been practising intercultural worship in one of the most culturally diverse cities in the United States, a context very different from Ian's in the UK. This difference is a benefit that enriches us, as we can learn from an author who has applied the same principles in a different setting. Learning about his experiences in the UK has broadened our perspectives and prompted us to re-examine our own assumptions and judgements.

No single person holds all the answers on this subject; diverse voices are essential in intercultural worship because every context is unique, not only the multicultural contexts that this book addresses. Not many authors can write about this emerging practice of intercultural worship because as yet not many have chosen to walk this journey. This book is answering the call of Jesus, who prayed for the unity of his followers as a powerful witness of God's love for the world. The biblical idea of unity is not uniformity but unity within diversity, as reflected in our triune God. God is preparing every tribe, tongue and nation to bring its own glory and honour to the wedding feast in the new kingdom as the Bride of Christ. We hope this book will serve as an incarnate presence of Jesus in diverse contexts worldwide, enabling and guiding churches not only to coexist but also to co-create as one family in Christ.

Joy Kim
Ethnodoxologist, Proskuneo Ministries

Jaewoo Kim
Ministry Development, Proskuneo Ministries

Acknowledgements

This book results from conversations and experimentations with wonderful people, many named in its pages. First, however, if this publication enables churches to express worship in ways that more fully honour our triune God, its purpose will have been achieved. With that in mind, I acknowledge Osman Kamara, whose worship contributions launched Oldham Family Church's journey into intercultural worship. Thanks, also, to the big-heartedness of its elders and members.

I salute Matt Hatch, a first reader of this book, and Dan Chadwick, both leaders in Mosaic Church, Leeds, for their inspiring steps to embrace intercultural church and worship. Izibongo and *Aradhna*, your worship leading helped me see excellence in multicultural worship!

I honour the leaders of the Global Consultation on Arts and Music in Missions and the Global Ethnodoxology Network, all heroes, including Dr Brian Schrag, whose co-creation methodology lies behind this book, and Dr Robin Harris, who encouraged me to amplify Brian's principles for multi-ethnic congregations.

Special gratitude goes to Dr Jill Ford for her perception, early on, that 'this is what we need' at All Nations Christian College, where I have especially developed this material, and to Revd Dr Warren Beattie, who has sharpened my writing, including this volume, along with Anne Soh, also a first reader. I thank all my students and fellow tutors at All Nations, London School of Theology, the Worldview Centre for Intercultural Studies, Australia, as well as Revd Dr Jacob Joseph and students at New Theological College, India, whose interactions have honed my thinking. I thank every leader of WEC

AN INTERCULTURAL WORSHIP HANDBOOK

International, for believing in this vision with me, and of Arts Release and Resonance, for developing this with me.

I extend appreciation to Graham Kendrick for his kind Foreword, and for courageously inviting me to address a group of worship songwriters in 2008, as well as Les Moir and the Imagine forum, all of whom have spurred my vision.

Theo and Rieneke Visser, Adam Martin, Jessie Tang and Songs2Serve are fellow pilgrims on this path, as are Josh Davis and Proskuneo Ministries, including Jaewoo and Joy Kim, with their perceptive comments on an earlier manuscript, and now a Foreword.

Thank you, Canterbury Press, for believing in this book!

Finally, big hugs to my family, Ruth, Jo and James, Aaron and Rue, and especially my wife Helen, who have endured my self-doubts, questions and hesitations, and have been an untiring support in bringing this book to completion.

Ian Collinge

List of Tools

Chapter 1	Twelve Biblical Themes with Implications for Intercultural Worship (p. 4)	
	To connect biblical principles to practice	
Chapter 2	Influences on Our Sense of 'Culture' (p. 16)	
	To stimulate personal intercultural conversations	
Chapter 4	Twelve Motivations for Intercultural Worship (p. 35)	
	To think through strategic goals and priorities	
	Six Approaches to Worship Music in a Multi-Ethnic Church (p. 41)	
	To clarify current practice and an envisioned future	
Chapter 6	Heart Music Survey (pp. 84–7)	
	To understand others' deeply felt music preferences	
Chapter 7	Grid of Cultural Preferences in a Worship Meeting (p. 92)	
	To understand others' cultural expectations in worship	
Chapter 9	Possible Balance of Songs (p. 140)	
	One way to address unity and diversity in worship music	
Chapter 10	Developing a Shared Worship Culture (pp. 147–51)	
	Power dynamics and steps for becoming intercultural	
	Seven Lenses (pp. 152–4)	
	A wide range of factors to facilitate intercultural worship, including some typical worship meeting layouts	

Introduction

Lord, Change the Colour of Our Church!

'I'm looking for a church where I can play my drum', said Osman, arriving at the end of our church service with his five-year-old son by his side. Osman was an answer to prayer – a cry that had been offered that morning by church elders before the service: 'Lord, change the colour of the church to reflect the community around us!' It was a longing in our hearts. What we discovered was that Osman was Sierra Leonean, a nurse, a poet, a player of hand drums and a man who loved Jesus. He was one of a growing number of people seeking asylum in the United Kingdom and now located to Oldham by the Home Office. He lived just down the road from the community centre where our congregation met on Sundays.

The next Sunday, Osman brought his *djembe* drum and instantly added his sound to the songs for that day, songs common among British churches in the early 2000s. A few weeks later our church leader, Steve Alliston, invited Osman to teach us a song from Sierra Leone. His choice was, 'He's a miracle-working God', a song we could all sing in English. Later we tried 'Tel Am Tenki', a song in Krio, the trade language of his homeland. Osman started inviting other Africans to our church and they showed us how to sing and dance praise songs in Swahili and Luganda. Later, Iranians found us and then two Nigerian families arrived from Italy, as well as a Zambian family, so we learned songs in Yoruba, Bemba and Farsi – all with English versions. Osman arrived in mid-2002 and although none of us realized it at the time, it marked the beginning of a six-year journey.

This typically Caucasian (or 'white')[1] British congregation moved from being totally monocultural in people and worship to becoming a culturally diverse church of at least eleven nationalities, whose worship was increasingly intercultural, gradually reflecting who we were. In 2007 the local newspaper ran an article about us entitled, 'Cosmopolitan church, one big happy family' (Barker, p. 8).

It was a step-by-step journey that did not happen overnight. We stumbled. We wobbled. We made too many assumptions. But there was a lot of love between church members. It required an openness to do things differently and, looking back, we can see that it was a path guided and enabled by the Holy Spirit. And – the church grew in more ways than one.

Who is this Book For?

This book is for you if you have a passion to encounter the reality of 'every nation, tribe, people and language' (Rev. 7.9) worshipping God together, wherever you are. For example:

- You're keen to move into intercultural worship but need guideposts.
- You have already started out but want encouragement and tools.
- You're not totally convinced but want to check out what an increasing number are eager to explore.

It is for anyone who sees intercultural worship as a space where we can worship together with *one voice* (Isa. 19.23; Rom. 15.6) and with *diverse expressions* (Rev. 21.26). This desire arises because we know Jesus levels the ground between cultures and we want to be able to stand in the presence of God as equals (Gal. 3.28). At the same time, you know there are hurdles to navigate. If so, you are not alone!

---

[1] Throughout this book I generally use the term 'white' rather than 'Caucasian'. This follows terminology in the UK Census 2021, which covers several sub-classifications of 'white'.

INTRODUCTION

I believe this topic is relevant across the world because I have worked cross-culturally for many years. While many examples cited here come from the UK, the undergirding biblical and best-practice principles are applicable for any multi-ethnic worshipping community – though local contexts vary greatly. Indeed, global events and developments of the past decade have brought to the foreground the question: 'Does our current worship style accidentally sideline some people?' Such events include migrations, people-trafficking, wars, poverty, financial instability, the coronavirus pandemic and climate pressures. The murder of George Floyd in the USA accentuated a new level of interracial conversation among church leaders, spotlighting concerns around race, cultural diversity and the colonial legacy of some European nations. Some leaders became aware of the mismatch between the various cultures attending church and their often monocultural worship practices. All these raised the hope of doing worship more respectfully of others. Many now conclude that culturally diverse worship can no longer be ignored. If that is you, may you find that this book gives you fresh courage.

My main focus is on worshipping communities that are already ethnically diverse. However, even for mono-ethnic congregations sharing a common language, there are reasons for expressing some cultural diversity: maybe a desire to anticipate the eternal vision of worship, to pray for other nations or to give a voice to minority groups. For such churches, ventures into 'intercultural worship' may be occasional but stimulating. The guidelines offered here should help to plan such events. For other contexts where intercultural worship principles can also work, see Appendix 2.

A Handbook

This book is intentionally practical because I do not aim to raise false hopes by reinforcing a glorious vision without some help along the way. It is a handbook with tools to use.

Routes

There is no one route into intercultural worship, because each church is unique in its character, history, memories and people. Your starting point and likely 'destinations' are specific to your situation even if they share similarities with others. For this reason, this book points to landmarks to notice and ways to plot your own adventure.

Tools

Some of the tools in this book are practical, highlighted by 'action icons' or by shaded text boxes. Others are lists, graphics and surveys you can use at different points where they are helpful.

Here I will highlight three. First, I have developed a diagram of 'Six approaches' that I have used over many years (p. 41). It depicts common approaches by multi-ethnic churches to cultural diversity in worship that can suggest a route between your present reality and your God-given hopes. Second, a 'heart music' survey (pp. 84–7) will help you discover a range of musical options for your church. Third, the 'Grid of cultural preferences' (p. 92) in worship shows how culture more generally impacts people in worship. These tools are designed to help make informed creative decisions about priorities.

Guideposts

This book also provides a set of guideposts. First, the structure of the book loosely follows an increasingly influential ethnodoxological process called Creating Local Arts Together, drawn up by Dr Brian Schrag,[2] who has welcomed its use for this book. This model uses a set of seven interlapping conversations to guide a given community to specify goals and select artistic ways to help meet those needs. Here the process is applied to a church community. Second, there are

---

2 Used with permission. A second edition with revisions is now available.

INTRODUCTION

theological principles and biblical texts that undergird my approach. These are our guideposts.

Allow me to illustrate the need for guideposts from personal experience of walking the three-mile pilgrim route barefoot across the sands from the coast of Northumberland, North-East England, to Holy Island.[3] Tall posts, about forty paces apart, show the safest route. Without these markers you can quite literally get stuck in the mud because, for much of the day, the island is cut off from the mainland by the sea. You can only safely walk across when tides are out, following the route taken by monks in the seventh century AD when the island was the centre of Celtic Christianity in England. This legendary location retains a sense of mystery and, for me, walking with pilgrim companions across this in-between space turned out to be a sacred experience. We were clearly warned to 'Stick to the guideposts'! Soon enough we encountered pools of water, seaweed and very slippery sections where you can easily lose a shoe (if wearing any) in the mud. It is tempting to think that you can identify a better way but the posts really do indicate the best route. Jeremiah advises:

> ask for the ancient paths, ask where the good way is, and walk in it, and you will find rest for your souls. (Jer. 6.16)

In the same way, there are waymarkers for us to follow for intercultural worship. I believe that if you make use of these you will overcome many obstacles. How so? First, these are time-tested 'ancient paths', founded on secure scriptural foundations for building intercultural relationships. Second, I have worked across cultures for much of my life and there are some best-practice principles I have picked up from others – and from my own mistakes! Third, I have been developing multicultural worship music for over 20 years, have noticed where some of the pitfalls lie and have sought ways to navigate around them. My hope is that you will not have to get stuck in similar places. Fourth,

---

3 Also known as Lindisfarne. For more see: Northumberland Coast National Landscape, 2024, *Pilgrim's Way to Holy Island*, https://www.northumberlandcoastaonb.org/pilgrims-way/ (accessed 3.12.24).

others have gone before us, planting excellent guideposts, and I present the combined wisdom of multi-ethnic worship practitioners. In short, the aims of this book are to give confidence that the journey is possible, to point to established routes, to offer help and provide extra motivation to keep going at potential sticking points.

The Vision: A New Sound

I began this journey in Asia in the mid-1990s when I lived in Nepal, conducting ethnomusicology research. I discovered how believers from ethnic groups in the Himalayas worship Jesus more naturally. This opened my eyes and ears to ways of expressing praise that are profound and beautiful – yet quite different from British approaches. They exhibit the God-given strengths of that culture. By 2002 we were in Oldham, Greater Manchester, and our church started attracting asylum seekers and other migrants. Since then I have been pursuing culturally diverse worship in local churches. Then, in 2008, God spoke to me about a 'new sound' that needed to emerge in UK Christian worship – a sound representing the variety of peoples who make up God's church here. I had no idea how this would come about but felt God prompting me to be a voice for multicultural worship, conversing with and listening to others, reading, teaching, writing and consulting about it. I later started the Resonance Band to inspire and equip interested leaders and congregations. In my local church, Mosaic Church, Leeds, there is an intentional commitment to make intercultural church and worship happen, bringing nations together and elevating the voices of people from diverse cultures. It's changing the way we see things – an increasing number of church leaders are eager to break into the Revelation 7.9 vision of 'every nation, tribe, people and language', standing as cultural equals before God in worship. I believe intercultural worship is the rising voice of the church for the coming generations.

INTRODUCTION

A Journey with the Holy Spirit

To help make sense of this, let us be inspired by the prophet Ezekiel's vision of the valley of dry bones (Ezek. 37). Here, God speaks to Ezekiel concerning the people of Israel at that time – that he wants to bring them to life from their metaphorical 'death' in exile. Professor Steven M. Bryan describes it in this way:

> *When asked if a nation that had died could yet live, Ezekiel equivocates: it would take an extraordinary act of God. But the NT [New Testament] insists that this is exactly what happened in the death and resurrection of the Messiah. (Bryan, Point 8)*

Indeed, there was an 'extraordinary act of God' – through the work of Christ – in which he brought into being the church of Jesus Christ: one people from many people groups. This encourages us that God desires to work in our communities – doing things that we cannot bring about on our own. In this analogy of the dry bones, let me propose that Christ's church can be 'asleep' (or 'dead') to the fuller vision Jesus has for it. Often we have become stuck in our culturally predictable ways of doing things and may even lack the imagination to become the type of church we want to be. We are clearly not alive to the beauty, the richness, the eye-catching potential and the depths of intercultural unity that can be ours when we unlock the stories, the sounds, the colours, the rhythms, the poetry, the passions and everything else that reflects the glorious image of God in human cultural diversity – and is waiting to be released into Christian worship.

Like Ezekiel's dry bones, we really need God's Spirit to enable us to become a church shaped by a vision not of separate kingdoms, but of God's kingdom. This is also the promise of Pentecost. Come, Holy Spirit, open our eyes to what we do not yet see; put fresh fire in our hearts and move us to glorify Christ, the head of his multicoloured body, for:

> *Here there is no Gentile or Jew, circumcised or uncircumcised, barbarian, Scythian, slave or free, but Christ is all, and is in all. (Col. 3.11)*

Multicultural or Intercultural?

First, however, a few words about words. You may be thinking that 'multicultural', 'multi-ethnic', 'multiracial' and 'intercultural' worship are simply different ways of talking about the same thing. Well ... yes and no! I love the way Mohan Seevaratnam put it in an interview:

> *We deliberately use the word 'intercultural' rather than 'multicultural' because it's possible to live in a multicultural society where cultures coexist alongside each other but still have little meaningful interaction. However, in an intercultural community, values are proactively shared. We enjoy mutual learning and blessing from each other's cultural insights. (Seevaratnam)*

On its own the term 'multicultural worship' merely implies variety – that *something* is multicultural. Some use it to indicate that their *people* are multicultural while admitting that their worship is still *monocultural*. Other uses mean that different *languages* are used. Strictly speaking, that is 'multilingual worship'. A more accurate use is where a congregation sings songs, prays prayers and conducts various aspects of a service that represent different cultures. But we still may not know how this connects to people's relationships, nor who is involved in decisions about worship. We could therefore describe multicultural worship as:

> People of multiple cultures represented together in Christian worship, using culturally diverse forms.

They may be 'represented' but not consulted! By contrast, 'intercultural worship' means all the above and more. It means that our shared multicultural worship expressions arise out of deep intercultural

INTRODUCTION

interactions. The 'inter-' bit speaks of inter-human communication. Therefore intercultural worship could be explained as:

> People of multiple cultures interacting together to develop worship expressions that represent them all in deeply meaningful ways, as cultural equals.

'Multicultural', then, emphasizes difference. We can enjoy this but there is a risk that it becomes a variety show or a box-ticking exercise. 'Intercultural', however, emphasizes relationships, community, equality and shared voices. There is a catch here. We might develop fantastic relationships but, surprisingly, we might not go as far as expressing our diversity in worship! Therefore we need both multicultural and intercultural approaches. Together, they help us develop a 'heaven on earth' atmosphere. On the other hand, only an intercultural approach will avoid the pitfalls of the multicultural, such as awkwardness, tokenism, cultural appropriation and cultural superiority. So in this book we will focus on the 'intercultural', because it speaks of the importance of our two priorities for other-affirming worship: intercultural listening (deep, humble and intentional) and intercultural experimentation (humble, collaborative, creative).

Maybe it would clarify things to express it in this way:

> Intercultural worship is not only about adding something to our existing worship. It is where growing together results in our worship becoming something new.

This brings us back to our reliance on the Holy Spirit to create something new among us. Intercultural worship is, in essence, a congregation's corporate, communal and community-shaped response to God's revelation in Christ. It is therefore radically countercultural since it opposes highly individualized, consumerist or highly tribalized worship, whether this is an ethnic, generational or subcultural 'tribe'. Instead, it fosters a shared worship culture that takes account of the church's history, its predominant culture and language, worshippers' languages and cultures and cultivates a passion to express that in intercultural ways.

Race, Ethnicity and Culture

Race

It would be easier to avoid terms like 'Black', 'White' and 'Asian' because of potential misunderstandings, but I have chosen to use these, following the UK government's primary categories for 'ethnicity' in the UK Census 2021. In their book *Healing the Divides*, Jason Roach and Jessamin Birdsall wisely admit that:

> *Another tricky thing about the current conversation around race is that there are lots of key terms that people define differently. (Roach and Birdsall, p. 16)*

But they go on to say that we need to 'continue to use terms such as "race", "racial" and "racism" … because [race] has had, and continues to have, major implications for the ways in which people are seen and treated' (p. 18). In other words, by ignoring terms based on physiological differences we run another risk: that of ignoring the emotional and societal impact of racial prejudice, abuse, stereotyping, superiority and indifference – including in the church. Intercultural worship provides a space where churches can address such things in a spirit of love and openness.

Nations and Ethnicities

Roach and Birdsall also point out that 'ethnicity' provides more of a biblical understanding (p. 18). In the Bible, there is one 'human race' (p. 29; see also Acts 17.26) with many nations, peoples and ethnic groups. In Christ, believers are one people (Eph. 2.14–22; 1 Pet. 2.9–10). The potential for intercultural worship therefore starts here. Our sense of ethnic identity usually connects to stories we and those in our more recent history have told. Taking a chronologically long view, Professor Alice Roberts helpfully describes how a search for our identity through DNA and family history is unlikely to result in a single ethnic identity, due to the continual movements of people for millennia. Instead, our ethnic identity is usually socially and culturally constructed:

> *Ethnicity is not a biological phenomenon, even if it might draw on some biological features like eye, hair and skin colour. We construct it based on our recent ancestry, on the place in which we were born, the place in which we live, a particular set of values and rituals – which may or may not be associated with a religion, the language we speak and the stories that we tell.* (Roberts, pp. 268–9)

Culture

Lastly, with intercultural worship we naturally recognize 'culture'. This is 'a set of beliefs, values, practices, styles and narratives that provide people with a sense of meaning and belonging' (Roach and Birdsall, p. 164). None of these is fixed. They develop over time. Culture, therefore, is fluid and, for multicultural churches, this is very positive. It means that gradual changes in the ways we see and do things are not only possible but natural, especially when we allow the Holy Spirit to lead us.

My Background and Hopes for this Book

I fully acknowledge that a book like this is limited by the experience and understanding of its author, and so I apologize in advance for any defects, misrepresentations, blind spots and mistaken assumptions. I also recognize that there are reasons why churches adopt other models in favour of an intercultural approach (Whitesel, pp. 22–35; Van Velden). Having said this, I hope that this book will be a useful contribution to ongoing discussions about intercultural worship.

In my early years, I was shaped as a white British person raised in Church of England schools and choirs. As a young adult, I was a violin teacher, attended a Baptist church and theological college and was called on to pastor a new church in London. I have since spent 35 years engaging with people of other cultures as an interdenominational, cross-cultural missionary, ethnomusicologist and ethnodoxologist and, most importantly, as a fellow worshipper of Jesus. This included 20 years focused in or on Asia, engaging with people of cultures and world views very different from my own. I have facilitated songwriting workshops and have learned the importance of each group having agency to develop worship music in ways that their own background and aspirations suggest. As for intercultural worship in England, I have been involved in Newfrontiers churches for over 20 years, two of which have intentionally experimented with intercultural worship. And I have had the privilege of ministry in churches from a range of racial, cultural and denominational backgrounds. I therefore believe that principles in this book can apply across continents and traditions. Many churches in Europe are small to medium in size (30–300 adults), sometimes with few resources. They not only attract ethnic groups well established in Britain but also recently arrived people from a very wide range of backgrounds, representing between several to over 100 nationalities. I trust that the many examples and suggestions will inspire you to press on with your vision for culturally diverse worship.

Questions to Ponder

1. How open is your church or organization to cultural diversity in worship?
2. How would you explain to another person the difference between 'multicultural worship' and 'intercultural worship'?
3. How might these distinctions help to clarify what your church/organization is doing or could be doing?

1

Seeing:
Vision and Motivations

*The hand of the L*ORD *was on me, and he brought me out by the Spirit of the L*ORD *and set me in the middle of a valley; it was full of bones. He led me to and fro among them, and I saw a great many bones on the floor of the valley, bones that were very dry. (Ezek. 37.1–2)*

What Do You See?

Ezekiel's vision of the dry bones starts with two things: God's hand moving him and Ezekiel seeing something new. What do you 'see'? What is driving you towards intercultural worship? One answer might be cultural diversity in society and church. While percentages for minorities in Scotland are lower, census figures show that the UK population as a whole is becoming more diverse. Indeed, a 2021 report states:

> *It is estimated that by 2050, 30 per cent of the UK population will be from an ethnic minority background, up from 11 per cent in 2010. As the UK grows in diversity, there is a need to better understand how the UK Church is – and is not – effective in crossing cultural, racial, and ethnic barriers. (Eido Research, p. 1)*

There are still many churches with no one from ethnic minorities but their number is decreasing. A Methodist congregation in a small former mining town in County Durham recently experienced this when an Iranian family arrived. To their credit, this church immediately started projecting words in Farsi and English to help the Iranians engage in worship. Other regions and countries may also expect population change. The church needs to respond to this changing reality.

First and foremost, however, the church derives its primary vision for church life from the scriptures that highlight God's love for the nations, that he desires us to love one another and that it is by his enabling grace that the miracle of intercultural worship can happen. For a biblical vision, most church leaders point universally to Revelation 7.9, where 'a great multitude that no one could count, from every nation, tribe, people and language' worships God in the new heavens and new earth. We will look at this below, since it is perhaps the single most powerful motivator for this vision, but we will also examine a range of other biblical motivations that feed into our vision.

The picture of culturally diverse worship in eternity creates excitement – but even if we do not often see it in our churches, let us not lose heart. This sense of longing might itself be the sign of God stirring something in our hearts! Looking again at Ezekiel's dry bones, we note that what was missing in his vision was *life*. He saw an army of unmoving and lifeless corpses. The passage shows a four-stage process:

1 God moves in us and speaks: we become aware of something (inspiration).
2 The bones come together: people connect and 'rattle' with each other (dialogue).
3 Flesh is added: the skin, flesh and tendons become attached (collaboration).
4 The Holy Spirit brings it all to life (transformation and newness).

In this book we will see each of these but it starts with God speaking into our hearts (Ezek. 37.1). Like Ezekiel, we might say 'the hand of the Lord was upon me'. What is God putting on *your* heart? It is only a vision from God that will energize us sufficiently to change our practices and keep motivated on the way.

Biblical Foundations

There are numerous passages that, put together, speak of a keen desire in the heart of God for diversity, beauty and the preferring of others above ourselves in worship. The following list of twelve is just a sketch. Let's start with the end-picture in Revelation 7.9–10:

> *After this I looked, and there before me was a great multitude that no one could count, from every nation, tribe, people and language, standing before the throne and before the Lamb. They were wearing white robes and were holding palm branches in their hands. And they cried out in a loud voice: 'Salvation belongs to our God, who sits on the throne, and to the Lamb.'*

This picture evokes a longing to gather around God's throne with all those he has redeemed from across the earth through time (also Rev. 5.9–10), to declare his worth together. It fuels a desire for a kaleidoscopic range of worship here on earth. Sometimes we sense this in large international meetings. Even in small churches or watching a screen, we find ourselves caught up in a global movement that encompasses the nations. One musical example might be the global cover of 'Nara Ekele Mo' by the Resonance Band, eliciting YouTube reactions such as, 'A Taste of heaven ... Every race, language and tribe singing praise to God ... beautiful' and 'This is a true expression of Multicultural music.' The 'taste of heaven' experience is probably the reason why Revelation 7.9 is almost always the verse that comes top of the list.

After this, other scriptures come to people's minds, such as Psalm 96.1, 7:

> *Sing to the* LORD *a new song;*
> * sing to the* LORD, *all the earth.*
> *Ascribe to the* LORD, *all you families of nations,*
> * ascribe to the* LORD *glory and strength.*

The list we now come to suggests that, from Genesis to Revelation, the whole Bible speaks of God's love of diversity and unity. This includes his design for the nations to spread out across the earth, to develop languages and cultures and that his blessing will come when we seek him in unity (Ps. 133). Jesus not only gave honour to non-Jews and commissioned his followers to disciple all nations, but on the cross he abolished the 'dividing wall' between God and humanity and between people groups (Eph. 2.14). Jesus prayed for his disciples to demonstrate unity – to reflect the oneness that has eternally existed in the community of the Godhead (John 17.23). No wonder the picture of the eternal city is of unity with mind-spinning diversity (Rev. 21.15–27).

In the list below we reflect on twelve key biblical principles and take note of what implications each of these has for intercultural worship. Texts, along with implications for worship, are provided in note form. If you teach on this topic, you would do well to make a fuller, in-depth study of these verses.

Twelve Biblical Themes with Implications for Intercultural Worship

1 **All cultures reflect God's image: Gen. 1.26–27**

   God created human beings in his *image*.

   Implications: human cultures therefore reflect God's image in unique ways. However imperfectly, each adds to our understanding of God.

2 **God made all the nations: Gen. 1.28; 11.8–9; Ps. 86.9**

   God created nations (ethnic groups) and languages.

   Implications: culture and language groups communicate God's truth differently. This diversity is enriching.

3 **God made all nations to worship: Ps. 86.9; 96.7**

   God desires *every* nation to worship him.

   Implications: all human cultures can worship and should be encouraged to bring their own worship to God.

4 Nations are to worship together: Isa. 19.23–24

God desires the nations to worship him *together*.

Implications: God desires to be worshipped by people together, regardless of divides, even when these groups have traditionally been fierce enemies (as with the Assyrians, Egyptians and Jews).

5 All nations should be discipled to worship: Matt. 28.17–20

All ethnic groups are to be discipled (v. 19) and disciples *worship* God (v. 17).

Implications: all ethnicities are to be discipled to worship. The content of Christian worship is the same (Father, Son and Spirit: v.19), although cultural expressions of worship differ.

6 Multilingual worship: Luke 24.45–53 (esp. 47, 53); Acts 1—2

The Holy Spirit enables disciples to witness to all nations and to worship God from their heart.

Implications: *multilingual* worship is desired and empowered by God. It is a form of witness to those who understand those languages (Acts 2.11).

7 Acceptance of the other is worship: Rom. 15.1–11

Believers in the early church in Rome are to please one another (v. 2), live in unity (v. 5) and accept one another (v. 7) in order to glorify God with one heart and one voice (v. 6) and to praise him (v. 7).

Implications: intercultural worship is the biblical *norm*. An other-affirming approach to worship stands against our own cultural pride. It is possible in practice if believers from diverse cultures care enough to lay aside some cultural preferences so others can also express their voice.

8 Transcending cultural domination: Gal. 2.14; 3.26–28

Paul had to challenge Peter, saying, 'How is it … that you force Gentiles to follow Jewish customs?'

Implications: in an intercultural church, a fine balance needs to be found in worship between shared language and cultural forms (usually of the majority) and giving space for individuals and minority groups to express worship in unique cultural ways.

9 Multicultural early church: Acts 13.1; 1 Cor. 12.13; Eph. 2.19; 3.1; Col. 3.11

The church in many New Testament cities was cosmopolitan. Paul is alert to language, ethnic and class differences, including Barbarians and Scythians (non-Greek speakers), as well as Jews and Greeks.

Implications: believers of all languages, cultures and classes should be invited to *contribute* to worship (1 Cor. 14.26), expressing themselves in ways most natural to them. However, this is not a free-for-all. Paul exhorts order. Leaders need to guide how this will shape worship (1 Cor. 14.40).

10 Diverse worship in the early church: 1 Cor. 14.26; Eph. 5.19; Col. 3.16

The early church used culturally diverse *forms*: songs in a Jewish style, some that were Greek influenced and others that were spontaneous in a person's own style. Such songs undoubtedly reflected an individual's ethnic and/or musical background.

Implications: Christian worship will be intercultural if it is Spirit-led and flexible, representing not only historic traditions and forms from a dominant culture, but also the expressions of others present in worship.

11 Diverse worship in eternity: Rev. 5.9; 7.9

God's heavenly court includes worshippers from 'every tribe, language, people and nation'.

Implications: the New Testament vision for worship is *inclusive*, united, diverse and intercultural. No group is excluded. The book of Revelation was written for believers still living. Hence, this vision is to inspire worship now, 'on earth as it is in heaven'.

12 The best of human cultures in eternity: Rev. 21.22–27

The 'glory and honour of the nations' will be brought into the new heavens and new earth. The best and purest forms of all human cultures will find their place in the *eternal* city.

Implications: earthly worship can reflect the eternal vision of worship with a diversity of languages, cultural and artistic forms that demonstrates the kind of unity Jesus prayed for.

What Stands Out to You?

In the above list, what stands out as especially important to take on board for yourself or to communicate with others in fresh ways? This list is a tool that could be used in private or group Bible study and could inform sermons focusing on culturally conscious worship and liturgy. Similarly, it may help those who introduce songs to know how to encourage congregations when singing songs from the wider church. In our Oldham church, worship leaders realized the benefit of a sentence or two just before the song. The list could provide a helpful resource for these inspirational comments.

Worship is Intertwined with Culture

Worship is a spiritual activity but it is also deeply cultural. Culture is rather like the air around us: we usually only become aware of it when something changes in it – like a smell! But the air is always there. Similarly, every act, however spiritual, is shaped by the way we have learned to do things. That's culture. For example, on a month in the Hausa-speaking part of Northern Nigeria, our small group from England learned how greetings with people we met along the way included questions about health, tiredness, each family member in turn and about livestock. Inevitably, such exchanges take time and cannot be rushed. This is very important; it acknowledges the person's community and lifestyle. This stands in contrast to brief greetings in the United Kingdom. Similarly, *how* we worship Jesus and what we *prioritize* can vary enormously. For example, approaches to time differ. We might ask, 'In our church, what do we build our services around: punctuality, spontaneity or arriving at a sense of the congregation having met with God?'

Four Ways Christian Worship Relates to Culture

A very helpful statement addressing the relationship of worship and culture was drawn up in Nairobi, Kenya, in 1996 by the Lutheran World Federation's Study Team (LWF). They identified that 'Christian worship relates dynamically to culture in at least four ways' (pp. 22–9). These are summarized in the list below. If you are interested, please refer to the document itself for more in-depth analysis.

Relationship of Worship and Culture

1	Worship is *transcultural*, it has the same substance for everyone everywhere – it transcends culture.	Transcultural aspects include Bible reading, prayer, creeds, communion and baptism, some festivals, and so on.
2	Worship is *contextual*, varying according to the local situation (both natural and cultural).	Worship should be expressed in appropriate cultural forms, in ways that best communicate Christ.
3	Worship is *counter-cultural*, challenging what is contrary to the Gospel in each culture.	Worship should be a counter-cultural act that opposes all that stands against the lordship of Christ, including self and cultural or ethnic pride.
4	Worship is *cross-cultural*, making possible sharing between different local cultures.	Intercultural worship gladly shares across cultures and welcomes the riches that each culture brings to worship.

How does this help us on our journey into intercultural worship? First, it takes note of common transcultural functions and practices across all Christian traditions, regardless of culture, denomination and generation, such as the Bible, prayer and shared Christian practices. It does not do away with the core components of Christian worship established from the days of the early church. Simultaneously, intercultural worship is contextual: it is rooted in a local context and adapts to the God-honouring aspects of the cultures of those present. Third, the very act of intercultural worship is countercultural. It challenges the superiority of any culture and promotes 'looking to … the interests of others' (Phil. 2.4). It dethrones the idols of any group and exalts Christ. Fourth, intercultural worship crosses cultures through learning and experimenting together. Throughout this book, we will regularly be reminded of all four dimensions.

Having examined a vision for intercultural worship, we now need to take a close look at our church community (or the community the church seeks to reach). Knowing our community is vital in moving towards genuinely intercultural worship.

 Questions to Ponder

1 Of the twelve biblical principles, which (if any) points were new to you?
2 What are your most important principles for intercultural worship?
3 How could these biblical principles encourage you in intercultural worship?
4 Why is it important to consider how worship intersects with culture?

2

Bones:
Knowing Your Community

Examining the Community

Returning to Ezekiel's vision, we pick up the story:

> *I prophesied as I was commanded. And as I prophesied, there was a sound, and behold, a rattling, and the bones came together, bone to its bone. (Ezek. 37.7 ESV)*

What do these 'bones' symbolize? Verse 11 explains: 'these bones are the whole house of Israel' (ESV). In Ezekiel's day, the nation had for centuries been divided into two: the kingdoms of Judah and Ephraim. The bones, then, stand for 'the whole house of Israel', the historic twelve tribes. Later in the chapter, God reinforces this message, telling Ezekiel to join two sticks in his hand as a visual aid and to prophesy that God will reunite Judah and Ephraim:

> *'I will make them one nation in the land, on the mountains of Israel … they will never again be two nations or be divided into two kingdoms … I will put my sanctuary among them for ever. My dwelling-place will be with them; I will be their God, and they will be my people. Then the nations will know that I the LORD make Israel holy, when my sanctuary is among them for ever.' (Ezek. 37.22, 26–27)*

Unity of the tribes is God's intention today just as much as it was then. Two things naturally flow from this. First, God's people worshipping together is central to this unity, represented by 'the sanctuary'

(vv. 26–27). Second, united worship by previously separated communities is a powerful witness to the watching world that God is among them (v. 28). God's purpose to bring together the 'whole' people of God is, of course, is at the heart of intercultural worship.

Describing Your Church and Community

What are the 'bones' or 'tribes' that make up your church? What kinds of people are you? The following section is designed to encourage you to take a closer look at your church community from various angles. I have noticed that church and worship leaders are often very good at knowing their people. They must be, for all sorts of reasons. If that's you, you may be able to list answers to these questions very readily. But do not be too hasty – take a good look; some of these may require more investigation.

Questions About Your Church Life

Geography and Meeting Spaces

1 How does the geographical location of your church affect your church life, negatively and positively?
2 What are your physical and online meeting spaces? How could these be used to facilitate cultural diversity?

Ethnic Profile

1 What is the ethnic profile of the area where you meet (including home languages)?
2 How does that compare with the ethnic profile of your church?

Social and Economic Profile

1. What is the social profile of the surrounding community (such as economic and occupational factors)?
2. How does that compare with the social profile of your church?

Energy, Capacity and Attitudes to Change

1. What are your church members' energy levels, capacity to diversify and openness to change?
2. What are your church members' attitudes towards other cultures?

History

1. What is the history of your church and how does this affect your worship?
2. Where are the potential blocks? What could help open opportunities?

Leadership

1. What are your leadership styles and emphases (such as pastoral care, teaching, evangelism, strategy, prophetic insight or prayer)?
2. How could you maximize these to develop intercultural worship?

It could be helpful to start a document with this information, so that you can reflect with some clarity on your situation and your potential for developing new approaches. This will also help you to review your journey over time, when you look back on the route you have taken. As you respond to these questions, do not be overwhelmed by what seems insurmountable. Remind yourself that Ezekiel's vision is a picture of a miracle! God's desire is to bring the peoples together and he will help you; it is he who brings life.

New Testament Multi-Ethnic Churches

It is worth recalling that many New Testament churches were multi-racial and multi-ethnic. Paul's calls to unity and 'bearing with one another' (Eph. 4.2) in love are set in this context. With our worship focus in mind, the city of Colossae is a great example. Here in the Roman Province of Asia there were, at the very least, Romans, Greeks, Jews, Barbarians and Scythians. Other churches, like that of Antioch, clearly included black leaders (perhaps from North Africa) and people from Cyprus (Acts 13.1). Believers in Rome were likewise from a broad mix of cultures and economic backgrounds (evidenced by the names listed in Romans 16). Multiculturalism in the Christian church is no new phenomenon.

Exploring More About Cultural Identities

This section probes a little further into the ethnic and cultural make-up of your church. It aims to facilitate conversations about the breadth of your church members' worship forms. First, for intercultural settings especially, we should emphasize the error of making assumptions about anyone based on outward appearances and humbly acknowledge the importance of listening to our fellow believers' stories if we are really to understand them.

Second, a person's cultural identity can be extremely complex. For example, the Revd Anjali Kanagaratnam, a Church of England priest, was born in Sri Lanka but moved to the UK at the age of eleven. Her experience in the British church was welcoming and positive but she likens herself to a 'chameleon'. This is a commonly expressed process of learning to fit in and then, at some point along the way, a dawning realization of what is happening and the beginning of accepting one's multiple identities more fully:

> *I now realize that that little chameleon symbolized, in many ways, my own journey of faith and identity in the British church, a real-*

ization that was only evident through my formation at theological college on my way to ordination. It might seem strange for me to say that I had never really given much thought to my race throughout the three plus decades when I had worshipped and later ministered (as a Lay Minister) in the church in the UK. My family and I had found such welcome and love in the churches we worshipped in that our race was never considered to be an issue …

The change was gradual as God slowly but clearly showed me that I was a bit like that chameleon, changing myself to fit the surroundings. In one sense, we are all a bit like chameleons; we don't like to stand out, so we try our best to fit in. However, God showed me that my chameleon-like behaviour made me hide part of who I was and that when God calls us, he calls all of us. Keeping a part of my self hidden made me less authentic. (Kanagaratnam)

This experience of feeling the need to fit in is common and in a multi-cultural church the range of identities can be very broad. It is all too easy to overlook or oversimplify this.

Cultural Identities and Responses in Worship

Cultural identities of individuals include where they were born, where they grew up and perhaps especially where they went to school and established friendship groups. They are also affected by how long they have lived in different cultures, how deeply they integrated, what languages they speak and so on. If a person's sense of cultural identity (or identities) is complex, what can we do to grasp what is important for individuals and the congregation as a whole? Figure 1 is intended to enable church and worship leaders to identify some key areas to be aware of in conversation with people.

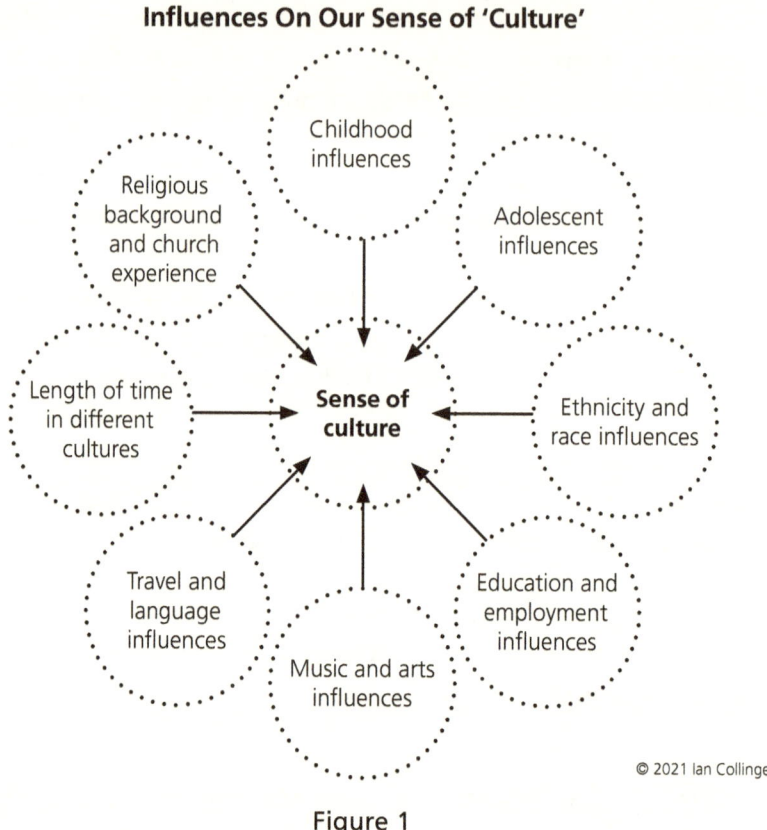

Figure 1

To illustrate how initial impressions may deceive us, let's consider a few examples. A mainland Chinese student expressed to me on several visits to our church that he loved the choral music of Johann Sebastian Bach. In the Mongolian world, I came across Mongolians for whom flamenco music is important. Similarly, African American Gospel music is a big thing in Japan (Fujino, pp. 274–8). Each of these musical preferences was developed while these people were living in their own countries. They show that we cannot assume that we will know anything about what will help a person in worship – until we interact with them.

At the same time, we can predict that the mix of people in a church will influence what music works for that congregation. A church largely attended by national and international students is likely to feel the need for very different expressions in worship from churches with middle-aged and elderly locals, and it will be different again for congregations of young families in areas with large immigrant communities.

Let's note some of the more obvious features that shape an individual's responses in Christian worship.

Childhood Influences

Childhood influences include our parents or care-providers, the society or societies in which we were brought up, especially the musical and artistic environment they created around us.

Adolescent Influences

Our teenage years are very important for exploring a sense of identity in relation to our peers. It is also a vital stage of life for musical exploration, when our 'heart music' is formed. We will look at this in a later chapter. For example, how come the Chinese student referred to above had a love for Bach's choral music? Was he hoping to find this being sung in our church? He explained to me that by the 2010s, western classical music had become popular among young people in Mainland China. The *South China Morning Post* journalist Christopher Halls agrees that 'appreciation for classical music in China continues to grow and mature, especially among young generations'.

Ethnicity and Racial Influences

Ethnic and racial background usually plays a significant role in our sense of culture. Music may (or may not) play a substantial part in this. For example, are there musical genres that we associate with personally in terms of our ethnicity or race? Jessie Tang compares music styles associated with three different groups in the UK:

> Where ... [Black British] ... in London have grime[1] and the South Asians have bhangra,[2] for example, the BBC [British Born Chinese] do not have their own musical style. (Tang, 2019, p. 8)

Musical identity based on place, race and community can be very specific. There is a pub-based English Christmas carol singing tradition in South Yorkshire and North Derbyshire, where different villages have preferred melodies for the same words (Russell, p. 81). This is loved by the community groups that foster it, including some of the younger generation. They sing in parts with full-throated enthusiasm. The folk singer Kate Rusby grew up with these carols and regularly includes 'Sheffield carols' in her Christmas albums – revealing an important part of her musical and cultural identity.

At the same time, I have found that the sounds and styles of music from a region with which a person identifies can have a profound effect on them, regardless of how much they actively engaged with these in their early years. Born in Sri Lanka, the Revd Ruwani Gunawardene was raised with western classical music and church traditions before living in England. After a time, this raised questions about her cultural identities in worship:

> All through this time, questions were rising within me as to how I could reconcile my culture with the worship culture in Britain. And the sounds that I had heard growing up, classical Asian sounds of sitar, violin, tabla and Sri Lankan drumming still pulled at my heart strings. I started to begin to feel that a part of me was missing and was crying out to be released.

She describes how hearing Asian sounds for the first time in Christian worship 'released' something within her. She speaks of two western

---

1 'Grime music is an innovative style of hip hop that originated in the UK in the early 2000s', see MasterClass, 7 June 2021, https://www.masterclass.com/articles/grime-music-guide (accessed 3.12.24).

2 'Bhangra originated from the Punjab region of India ... It is a fusion of Indian and Western music', see BBC Bitesize, https://www.bbc.co.uk/bitesize/guides/zkjw7p3/revision/1 (accessed 3.12.24).

musicians who 'mastered the Hindi worship traditions of … Mother India. This was a familiar sound, but not one I had *ever* associated with Christianity. Wow!'

These examples demonstrate that it is presumptuous to assume we know what musical worship style will help individuals. The 'heart music' survey later in this book is a tool to understand what music most readily unlocks the hearts of your church members to worship Jesus.

Religious Background and Church Experiences

Religious background affects us in many ways, including how music is used (or not). Persian non-Christians visiting churches in Europe, for example, are sometimes surprised that Christians express religion in song. For some, it is contrary to all they have so far expected in religion. Similarly, our church worship experiences can include denominational traditions as well as historic and global influences. The Sierra Leonean journalist and author Sheka Tarawalie ended up in Oldham, Greater Manchester. When he led in song, he demonstrated the influence of his church background on his personal worship culture when he introduced the hymn, 'What a Friend we have in Jesus'. Before singing it, Sheka related the songwriter's personal story behind the hymn in some detail. When I learned of Sheka's background in the Wesleyan Church of Sierra Leone, with its roots in the hymn-singing American Wesleyan Mission, I understood how his early churchmanship formed his heart music and established his worship preferences (Tarawalie, pp. 63–9).

Educational and Occupational Influences

Educational experiences can have an impact on our responses in worship, especially if the model is quite 'educational', such as in the Protestant tradition, where worship songs can be rich in text and sometimes in 'educated' language. This may be an attraction for some but can pose a barrier for others. People who struggled at school or do not know the congregation's worship language sufficiently well can be disadvantaged. In my experience, intercultural and multilingual worship can help to level the ground.

Employment and occupation also contribute to our identity. In Britain, a common question is: 'What do you do?' People often associate social status and self-worth with their occupation. How might this shape our worship preferences and language levels? These are questions worth exploring in conversations.

Musical and Artistic Influences

Our musical and artistic upbringing greatly affects our responses in worship. Our parents, caregivers, teachers and others provide the environment in which we learn to respond to music, poetry, theatre, visual art, books, film, digital media and so on. As adolescents and young adults, our peer groups often influence our tastes. This exposure in our younger years becomes deeply engrained, foundational to our responses to music and the arts – including worship – for the rest of our lives. It is commonly reported how people suffering memory loss often respond instantly to a song learned as children or young people. The Alzheimer's Association reports:

> *Even in the late-stages of Alzheimer's, a person may be able to tap a beat or sing lyrics to a song from childhood. Music provides a way to connect, even after verbal communication has become difficult.*

Intercultural worship, then, recognizes the deep level of connection that specific genres of music and the arts create in individuals and groups. In culturally diverse churches, a variety of musical and artistic forms is important to help people from a range of cultures, languages, generations and abilities to engage together in acts of corporate worship.

Travel and Language Influences

If we have travelled much and watch films and programmes featuring other countries, and especially if we have spent time in other cultures, learning local languages, we have a bank of global memories. Sometimes this opens us to diverse music and hence to other people's worship. Also, for those who speak other languages, there is usually much less fear of singing in diverse languages.

Length of Time in Different Cultures

Some people connect deeply to people from cultures other than their own passport culture and some grow up in an international school environment. The longer we spend in any culture the more at home we may feel. Some do not learn the local language because they already speak a language that many understand. Others take the time to learn the language and to communicate in culturally appropriate ways. All these experiences shape us in our sense of cultural identity.

In other words, the strength of need for one's heritage culture and language to be accepted in church varies greatly. For some new arrivals, the sense of loss is acute. Political refugees often face trauma and vulnerability. Churches who embrace aspects of these newcomers' forms of worship are simultaneously providing emotional and spiritual support in their adaptation to their new lives. Adults arriving in a new country with a secure job still find that settling can take years, and the need for their culture in worship can be strong, making it feel more like 'home'. Oldham Family Church welcomed many such people. Numerous things contributed to feeling welcomed by the church, especially practical help. However, one thing was common: although they were happy to join in with the existing worship, they were also keen to share their expressions of worship.

It is not always like that. Some may resonate with the experience of the Revd Anjali Kanagaratnam, who spent her formative years growing up in Britain, including in English churches. Like her, they may feel like a 'chameleon', presenting certain aspects of their identity in church and downplaying others, even if these are significant. They feel they need to leave something of themselves 'at the door' in worship led by the majority culture. That is where approaches found in this book may help. On one occasion, a group of us were invited to lead worship near Wakefield, Yorkshire. This congregation included an African lady and her children. For one of our songs, a team member started a processional 'conga' around the sanctuary. Afterwards, this lady confessed that she loved the freedom to express herself but had been on the verge of leaving the church in favour of an African-led church. Congregation members said she had always seemed restrained in services and were delighted to get a glimpse into this other side of her. In other words, she had left these important features of her cultural identity at the door. That day's experience encouraged her to stay; she saw that worship could be different in that church.

Others may feel less need for their own language or culture in church. They may speak the national language well, they may be very familiar with the worship style or are simply inquisitive. However, I have noticed that many still find it profoundly affirming to be asked to represent their language or background in some way. Yet others simply love musical and global diversity and, for them, cultural variety helps them worship.

But how do we discover what is important to people with such a range of cultural identities? We now come to the first of two pillars of intercultural worship: intercultural listening.

 Questions to Ponder

1 What countries, cultures and languages are present in your worshipping community?
2 How could using Figure 1, the 'Influences on our Sense of "Culture"' diagram, help your situation?
3 Does any example in this chapter resonate with your experience?

3

Listening: Where Intercultural Worship Starts

Intercultural Worship Starts by Listening Well

In this chapter our aim is to hear the worship longings of people in our churches. The reflections on identity in the previous chapter and the tools offered in this book are provided to help church leaders and musicians gain a fuller understanding of what kinds of worship expression will best serve their church.

At the heart of this is listening – listening attentively: a vital means to develop intercultural worship. Specialists in intercultural communication have coined various descriptors for this kind of listening, such as: 'loving', 'active', 'deep', 'compassionate' or 'humble' listening. In other words, this activity goes beyond hearing the words, to catch the 'heart' of the person. It is a skill that some learn professionally or in general life. It helps us avoid making assumptions and enables us to understand more truly. Others of us need to learn how to do this. The organization International Training Partners describes this as 'listening without judging or giving advice' (Williams, p. 15). As I have written elsewhere:

> *Such listening starts by openly acknowledging our own cultural ignorance, so that we can humbly learn from and 'value others above' ourselves … It begins behind the scenes but can then overflow into public acts of worship where all are honoured.* (Collinge, 2022a, p. 122)

Sahr Mbriwa expresses the journey of growth that may be involved in this kind of listening:

> *Listening well is difficult. It requires patience and effort, and it will require asking questions to better understand the context. This task is more difficult given that we listen best to what we want to hear, or to that which arises from shared convictions. James 1.19 speaks to this struggle to truly hear one another: 'You must understand this, my beloved: let everyone be quick to listen, slow to speak, slow to anger.'*

Significantly, Mbriwa goes on to say:

> *Listening will also cost you. It will not merely cost you time and energy, but loss of power. However long that moment might last, the one listening has in effect yielded to the one speaking. And if they are listening well, their mind is not elsewhere, but attentive to the other.*

Attentive listening is a Christlike activity, a cross-shaped practice. However, we should not beat ourselves up if we feel we are failing in this, but rather turn to the one who listens to the essence behind our every prayer, even our groans and sighs (Rom. 8.26–27).

 ## Listening to Objections

We also need to pay close attention to the objections and fears of those who feel uncomfortable with anything multicultural. The danger, of course, is that the objectors may drown out the voices of the under-represented. This is where we need great wisdom. Generally there are three common types of objections to intercultural worship: language, music and acceptability.

Language Objections

Some people feel that: 'Other languages are difficult'; 'I don't know how to pronounce the words'; 'I cannot understand the words'; and 'I cannot worship in another language'.

Admit the Problem

Mother-tongue English speakers enjoy a highly privileged position in the world. Their language is widely spoken, sung and written. Disconcertingly, however, this backfires on those who go along as happy English monoglots on the assumption that they do not need to try speaking even a few phrases in another language. A BBC report in 2015 said that a 'quarter of British holidaymakers feel nervous at the thought of having to speak the local language when they go abroad' (Sellgren).

Compare this situation with people in many other cultures who are accustomed, as a fact of life, to speaking a range of languages to various levels. For such people, 'having a go' at speaking or singing words in another language is quite normal. I have learned that it is usually more vital to boost the confidence of English speakers, encouraging them that they can sing and enjoy short phrases, than to do the same with people of many other cultures. A repeated response to times of worship led by the Resonance multicultural worship band is that people find themselves able to worship in other languages – and this includes Brits!

It's Not That Difficult

We shall address ways to use language in songs, prayer and other aspects of the service later in this book. Here I present some observations and questions.

Overcoming the Language Barrier

1. Try it. It is easier to sing in another language when imitating phrases and singing surrounded by others doing the same.

2. Arrange songs so that the amount of content in another language is enjoyable but not burdensome, such as short, repeated refrains. The rest of the song can be in the common language, such as English.

3. Use songs that are already multilingual. An example of this is 'Nara Ekele Mo', a song by the Nigerian Tim Godfrey, where the lead singer alternates between English and the Igbo language. Other than a short hymn-like section in English, the choir and congregation simply repeat three words: 'Nara ekele mo', which means 'Receive my thanks' (Godfrey).

4. Ask someone who can sing the 'other' language to take a lead or train others, as in the above song 'Nara Ekele Mo'. Then the whole congregation does not have to sing the more specialized bits.

5. Repeat it. The more a congregation sings a song, the more comfortable they will be with it.

Who Should Lead the Song?

Song leaders may feel that they are expected to learn all the lyrics in the relevant languages. This is not always the case and there are good reasons not to do so. Asking native speakers of the language who can lead the song is always the most respectful approach. They also often convey a feeling for the song and words that others cannot.

One Sunday morning, something marvellous happened when a colleague in a church in Manchester introduced 'I just want to say Baba O Ese', a bilingual song in English and Yoruba. He invited a Nigerian couple to the front to teach us the pronunciation. Instead of simply *speaking* the words, the wife started *singing* the song. The effect was electric! This lady caught the whole congregation up in her own worship. Suddenly people could feel her liberated praise. The hairs on my neck tingled and the congregation was so moved that they talked about this for months!

If a mother-tongue singer is not confident to sing, it is helpful to ask speakers of the language to teach the words to the lead singers or the whole congregation. Similarly, sharing the leading of songs broadens the scope to give people who are more confident or gifted in languages a chance to shine.

One Resonance Band member is especially attentive to the pronunciation needs of our songs, as well as having the voice of a nightingale. I found that native speakers of the song's language often came up to compliment her on the pronunciation of their language. Sometimes they assume that our singers also speak their language! But we need to be careful to do our best. If singing another's language is done with humility and sensitivity, mistakes can be easily tolerated if they see our desire to honour their culture.

It's an Act of Courtesy

If a congregation sings someone's language, it is an act of courtesy – a way of helping fellow worshippers to feel that they are welcome to play their part in the church on an equal footing. It is also a recognition of the multilingual character of Britain today. In 2017, Madeleine Davies wrote in the *Church Times*:

> *One in eight people in the UK were born abroad, and eight per cent have a tongue other than English as their main language. So churches are increasingly investing in ways to ensure that language is not a barrier to worship for the souls in their care. At the same time, they are reflecting on how to balance this with the need for integration.*

It is also worth acknowledging that those whose tongue is not the church's common language have to struggle all the time with pronouncing the words of our church's songs. It is humbling but powerful for the rest of the church to occasionally step into their shoes. It can have profound effects!

Abigail, a Zimbabwean lady, learned the Hindi song 'Amrit Vani' in a workshop. She then taught this song to the choir of her African-led church, which was neither Zimbabwean nor Asian. An Indian student nurse visited one Sunday, and hearing this song impacted the nurse so much that she brought along fourteen fellow Indian nursing students the very next week. Soon, one of these Indian women joined the choir!

Musical Objections

Musicians may think, 'Our music team is not good enough to play in different styles'; 'I'm not very good at my instrument, so I wouldn't know how to play that'; 'We don't have enough people on the worship team'; or 'Some multicultural worship songs are not easy to find on the internet'.

Smaller churches may face these issues more acutely if they do not have many musicians or resources. Conversely, larger churches are sometimes limited by the expectations they feel to present a certain quality of musicianship. However, 'Where there's a will, there's a way', as the saying goes!

Addressing Challenges of Musical Skill Levels

1 Find people who can add musical skills where they are missing, especially church members from other cultures.

2 Take it as an opportunity to learn what you can of other musical cultures, gradually and one step at a time. This may be a rhythm or a musical feature that at least one of the musicians can bring.

3 Let technology help. Play a video example of a song you want to feature. During Covid-19 lockdowns, some churches used online worship video materials featuring songs from the global church. This practice can also be included in services held in person.

4 Experiment in smaller contexts, practising together to develop new skills or to incorporate new members. Then you can take steps to integrate musicians and skills into your larger church settings.

Acceptability Objections

These reactions revolve around a fear that the congregation will not accept intercultural worship. People may say: 'Our worship is okay as it is; nobody will want to learn these songs'; 'We will lose people'; 'We won't be able to worship in the Spirit'; 'It will end up being a concert, not worship'; 'The majority culture will be marginalized and feel undervalued'.

Change Takes Time – Especially in Attitudes

The first responsibility of church leaders is to lay clear biblical foundations for any change they propose and to allay any fears that changes may somehow be wholesale and immediate. A gradual approach is always better for carrying more people along. In any change – and intercultural church worship almost always requires a shift in attitudes – some will be eager for change immediately, others will resist it and most will be happy to be taken on the journey step by step! Church leaders are aware that worshippers sometimes choose to leave in favour of another church. This is also true of intercultural worship. However, the rewards may turn out to be greater than the losses.

In Oldham Family Church, worship became intercultural over a period of several years and, remarkably, only one family left because of it. One family member wanted to worship in a church with people 'like me' rather than our cultural mix. In other words, they were an isolated case. For many, it was our growing multi-ethnic make-up that was attractive for Brits and non-Brits alike – and the church grew because of this.

Create an Appetite

A gradual approach will address different groups within the church. Opportunity for feedback along the way also allows for as many as possible to engage in the journey, to lay aside their concerns and to embrace new expressions with a positive outlook.

One of the best ways to create an appetite is to plan events that profile different cultures, perhaps of a more social nature, with food for example. These can happen outside of regular services. Alternatively, it is possible to drop 'appetizers' into regular meetings – a story, testimony, poem, song, reading or prayer led by brothers and sisters from these diverse cultures. Gradually these can be incorporated more into the main service. Connecting what we do to real people is a way for everyone to learn more about their fellow church members. In that way, while members of the church's majority group have a voice, they recognize that others need to be heard as well.

Keep it Spiritual

It is possible to sing any song and for our minds to lose focus. This is true of songs in other languages and musical styles too. The novelty of another language or style may in fact help us to keep our hearts focused. At the same time, it is also very easy for multicultural worship to feel like a variety show. It is the responsibility of the service leader and musicians to make wise decisions about when and how to incorporate such songs to make them meaningful. One way is to pair songs together – a well-known song with a new song on a similar theme or in a matching rhythm or key. Another way is to use songs from the global church for specific reasons, such as intercession or to highlight biblical truths in the readings, sermon or whole service. The secret is to keep the focus of worship spiritual.

In later chapters we will reflect on other kinds of resistance that leaders may face in moving into intercultural worship. For now it is good to note that, even from the word 'intercultural', we recognize the priority of interaction – of listening and learning – before and while we make any changes. Next, though, we need to listen to our own hearts, to clarify our goals and motivations.

 Questions to Ponder

1 What diversity of worship preferences have you already identified through listening?
2 What objections to intercultural worship are present in your Christian community?
3 In what ways can you develop your active listening skills?
4 What encouragements can you take away from this chapter?

4

Dreaming: What It Could Bring About

Identify Your Goals and Priorities

Why are you interested in intercultural worship? Why did you pick this book up? It is important to know because it will drive your decisions and direction, so we need to examine what really lies at the root of our desires to develop intercultural worship. There are many underlying reasons, some social, some spiritual, some theological, some civic, some to do with race, and many more. Identifying these is important because if you are clear about your chief goal, you are more likely to hit it!

In Chapter 1, we examined some of the biblical foundations for intercultural worship that inspire *vision*; in other words, *God's heart* for culturally diverse expressions, including worship. We focused on Revelation 7.9, Psalm 96 and twelve biblical principles with implications for intercultural worship. This is the big-picture aspect of vision. In this chapter, we turn our attention to the more immediate aspect of *our goals and motivations* for our church community. These will be concerned with specific issues in your context. Let's consider three examples and then expand the vista to examine twelve more, to assist in selecting one or two main priorities for your situation. Other motivations will then be able to support the key goal with greater force and effectiveness.

Three Examples of Goals

1 To 'Sing Ourselves into a New Reality'

This evocative phrase, drawn from Michael C. Hawn (p. 429), is an intentionally future-looking, prophetic stance. We want to bring our worship into line with an eternal vision and especially with our demographics – the specific communities of people we want to touch through worship. The *vision* is biblical but the goal is to attract these ethnic groups. It is *societal* and *evangelistic.*

Pastor Simon Pettit took this approach when deciding to adopt culturally diverse worship. As the then leader of Jubilee Church in Cape Town, South Africa, he saw a contradiction between their white majority church and the Xhosa- and Zulu-speaking communities around them. He instructed their worship leader, Evan Rogers, to sing two songs in other languages every meeting – to signal a welcome to people from these communities. And it worked! Evan writes that it felt strange at first: 'What seemed so false then has become natural now. We were seeking to be prophetic in our segregated society' (pp. 16–17; Lewendon).

2 To Welcome Refugees and Minorities

This second goal is for the church to be a place of welcome, especially for asylum seekers, refugees and minority ethnic groups. Over the past century there have been several waves of migration into Britain. In the 1960s the British church often did not welcome the many newly arrived Christians who tried to join; despite counter-examples such as the warm welcome the Sri Lankan Anjali Kangaratnam experienced later (see Chapter 2), racial prejudice was deep. Facing such hostility, diaspora ethnic congregations started, sometimes in desperation or anger. Generations later these emotional scars are still felt. As a result, some church leaders are determined never to repeat that tragic history and to act intentionally to tell an opposite story: that the church is a place of acceptance for all. These churches make it a point to welcome and include those of different races.

One such church is Anderson Baptist Church in Reading, England, a congregation with links to Nepal and a location close to a population of Nepalese, many connected to the British Army's Gurkha regiment. Now Alina Rai from Kathmandu is the minister and about half of the church numbers are Nepalese. Their recently retired minister, the Revd Judith Wheatley, speaks of equality of all races as a driving factor in their vision:

> *From the outset Anderson decided it wanted to be a church where everyone was an equal, not easy when there is a natural deference from one culture to another, particularly those with a Gurkha heritage. It has preached on Galatians 3 on numerous occasions, emphasizing that neither 'Jew nor Greek' also meant 'neither English nor Nepali'. This desire for equality, or a Christ culture, has impacted all aspects of life – leadership, worship, songs, prayers, seating arrangements, church meetings, finances, social gatherings and outreach activities. (pp. 19–20)*

3 To Help Society Address Issues of Racism

A third motivating factor is to combat societal racism. This has been a strong underlying reason for multi-ethnic church in the USA. In the UK it has been expressed more urgently in recent times. Robin Harris summarizes an account by Kersten Bayt, priest of 'an attempted church merger in South Carolina, between a congregation of Afro-American Independent Baptist tradition and one with an evangelical Southern Baptist tradition'. Harris draws attention to the social context behind this:

> *The pastors of these two churches proposed this merger in the context of heated public concern in South Carolina about church burnings and racially motivated hate crimes. In the public as well as the Christian arena there were strides being made toward reconciliation*

– the Southern Baptist Convention had recently apologized for its historic racism. The pastors of these two churches were convinced that 'desegregating the 11 o'clock Sunday morning hour' would be an important step in demonstrating that unity can be achieved. (2000, pp. 13–14)

Your Goals and Priorities

One of these three may or may not resonate with your aspirations, but take a close look at the following list to identify where your priorities lie. Many seem to overlap but, if possible, earmark one leading motivation (or a maximum of two) at the heart of your vision for intercultural worship.

1 To Reflect God

'Our vision for intercultural worship is to mirror something of the nature of God.'
Intercultural worship helps us reflect the dynamic diversity in unity existing first in the triune Godhead and then in humanity (Gen. 1.1, 26–27; John 1.1–3). Ours is a *theological* motivation – expressed through worship.

2 To Anticipate Eternity

'Our vision for worship is to anticipate the picture in Revelation 7.9.'
We want to worship in ways that promote deep communication with God and each other (Rom. 15.7; Mark 12.29–31; Rev. 7.9–10). Our goal is to value *contributions* in worship from all cultures in our church.

3 To Provide Welcome

'We see the need to create an atmosphere of welcome regardless of culture.'
Intercultural worship shows acceptance of new people in very visible ways (Rom. 15.5–11). Our goal focuses on *hospitality*.

4 To Foster Healing

'We want to create an environment of healing for asylum seekers and refugees.'
Many have suffered unspeakable traumas and are far from the familiarities and comforts of 'home'. We want minorities to feel heard and experience healing (Lev. 19.34). Our goal is *therapeutic*.

5 To Equip for Outreach

'We want to be better at reaching people of other cultures.'
Intercultural worship helps us build cross-cultural skills, giving us bridges of communication (words, songs and stories) to share with people of other cultures (Acts 2.11; 17.28; 1 Pet. 3.15). Our goal is *evangelistic*.

6 To Address Injustice

'We want to promote a very tangible and visible atmosphere to address injustices.'
True intercultural worship demonstrates equality, helping us reduce inequalities and cross-cultural prejudice (Deut. 10.18; Prov. 14.31; Mic. 6.8). Our goal is *social and racial justice* where the church can demonstrate a countercultural, Christ-centred way to bring races together. This is countercultural because it addresses entrenched and unconscious structures, attitudes and behaviours through its approach to worship.

7 To Confront Spiritual Powers

'We want to confront spiritual forces opposed to cross-cultural harmony.'
Through intercultural worship we demonstrate to ourselves, the world and all spiritual powers that, on the cross, Christ has done away with racial, social and cultural divisions once and for all (Eph. 2.14–19; 3.6–10; Col. 2.15). Our goal is *spiritual*, since prayer, praise and the declaration of truth in worship are powerful in disarming strongholds (Acts 16.25–26; 2 Cor. 10.4–5).

8 To Build Reconciliation

'We want to establish a warm climate for genuine reconciliation.'
Intercultural worship helps us level the ground between people of diverse backgrounds (2 Cor. 5.18; Eph. 4.3; Phil. 2.1–4; Col. 3.11), engendering mutual understanding and relationships. Our goal is the *healing of the nations* (Rev. 22.2; Ezek. 47.12).

9 To Value People's Identity

'We want all people to feel valued regardless of their heritage and identity.'
Intercultural worship enables us to give honour to people whose personal and cultural identities are undervalued, unseen, mocked or marginalized (John 4.7–9). Our goal is *pastoral*, giving a voice to individuals.

10 To Learn Scripture

'We want to equip our church members to learn more deeply of scriptural truths.'
Each culture has unique perspectives. Intercultural worship gives us a wider range of songs, stories and expressions to understand, embody

and apply the truth (2 Sam. 6.14; Ps. 141.2; Col. 3.16; Rev. 21.26). Our goal is *engaging with scripture*.

11 To Promote World Mission

'*We want to highlight global issues and need resources.*'
Intercultural worship provides us with ways to focus on local and global mission, the least reached peoples, the world church, the persecuted church, global poverty and the environment (Ps. 24.1; Isa. 24.4–6; Matt. 28.16–20; Rev. 7.9). Our goal is about a *global vision*, developing our passion for issues in the world.

12 To Grow Spiritually

'*Intercultural worship broadens individuals' personal devotional life.*'
Intercultural worship equips us with diverse cultural expressions that church members can use for themselves (Col. 3.16; Eph. 6.18; Rev. 21.26). This goal is about *personal spiritual growth*.

Write Down Your Primary Goal

Which of the above best represents your aspirations? You may think that all or most of them could be important to you because of the wide range of benefits that intercultural worship can have. Any of these could be a focus at different times. For example, your main motivation may be racial justice or a concern for asylum seekers but sometimes you want a global focus. So there could be one or two main motivations but also secondary motivations. Having said this, selecting a top goal and two or three supporting goals can be beneficial in articulating your vision to the church, the musicians and, maybe, to yourself.

DREAMING

Why not pause right now to bring this again to God in prayer? If God is making something clearer to you, don't let it go. Seize the moment! As the Lord said to several of his servants, 'write it down' (Hab. 2.2). This will help crystallize your thoughts and you can return to it later. If your church decides goals in a group setting, you could use the listed motivations to seek God for a clearer sense of direction.

Like the kingdom of God, it is likely that your vision and goals for intercultural worship will expand as God does things. In our Oldham church our main motivation expanded from 'reflecting the community' to include 'ministering to asylum seekers and migrants' (to provide welcome and foster healing).

Describe Your Current Worship Practices

A church leader described a discussion he held with his worship team. He simply asked, 'How are we doing in our current worship?' and was delightfully surprised at the level of honesty. What a good example that is! Proverbs 24.6 says, 'for by wise guidance you can wage your war, and in abundance of counsellors there is victory' (ESV). The following are some questions to pose, maybe in a leaders' meeting.

Questions to Ask About Your Church's Current Worship Practices

General

1. What is our typical order of service?
2. What alternative patterns have we already tried?

Music

1. What musicians do we have, with what skill levels?
2. What ages or cultures are represented in the music group (or choir)?
3. What musical styles are currently in use?
4. Which cultures' songs are used now?
5. Do we use any songs written by church members?
6. What openness is there by musicians to learn or use other musical styles?

Languages

1. What speakers of other languages are there and what languages are they?
2. What languages are currently used in worship?
3. How are these languages used?

Other Components

1. What non-musical forms of worship do we use?
2. What other arts do we use in church services?
3. What movement, dance or significant gestures are used?

Tracking Development

1. Have we recently sought feedback on our worship practice?
2. Does our current worship help move us to becoming culturally more diverse?

I suggest you take note of your answers, adding them to any document you may have already started in Chapter 2. What follows is an opportunity to use an earlier diagram (Figure 1 in Chapter 2) to help you ask: 'Where are we now and where could we aim for?'

Six Approaches to Worship Music in a Multi-Ethnic Church

There are many variant forms but I have observed six overall approaches to worship in a multi-ethnic church and found it useful to develop and refine the following diagram (Figure 2) over many years (Collinge, 2014, pp. 438–42; 2022a, pp. 129–38).[1] It is designed to prompt reflection and conversations to help you examine your worship through the lens of cultural diversity.

Six Approaches by Churches to Diverse Cultures in Worship

Monocultural	Multi-Congregational	Multicultural
Majority: 'Sing our songs'	'Sing your songs in your own groups'	'Sing your songs for us'
'assimilation'	'separate worship'	'rotational'

Intercultural	Intercultural	Intercultural
'Let's sing one another's songs'	'Let's create/arrange songs together'	'You lead, we'll support, in turns'
Integration	Innovation	Illumination
'blended'	'fusion'	'collaborative rotational'

○ Culture group   ♪ Worship styles in church   ☐ Church   ⬭ Interaction

© 2024 Ian Collinge

Figure 2

---

[1] In our present version I have renamed Approach #6 'Illumination', previously labelled 'Involvement' (Collinge, 2022a, p. 130, 137–8) or 'Initiative'.

Identify Your Starting Point

Your church may represent one of the six approaches mentioned here.[2] On the other hand, yours may be none of them, a variant or a mixture. But it is good to know where you are now in the light of who holds cultural privilege and who you give cultural preference to. Please note that we are specifically looking at *music* (hence the music note in Figure 2), to examine how it relates to the presence of multiple cultures in the congregation, but we can also use this approach to examine other facets of worship.

1 Monocultural Inheritance

In this multi-ethnic church, worship is monocultural. The majority cultural group makes the choices about music and other groups fit in. Some people call this the 'assimilation' approach (Whitesel, p. 34; Black, 2000, p. 92). The leading ethnic group *inherits* and sources its music from those it trusts to represent it culturally, denominationally or through the Christian media.

2 Multi-Congregational Independence

This church or group of churches resolve the question of diversity by conducting separate worship in relatively *independent* fellowships.[3]

3 Multicultural Inclusion

Churches practising multicultural inclusion invite members of diverse ethnic groups to lead songs in their own style, such as their own language, in a deliberate attempt at *inclusion* into the regular service. Some call this the 'rotational' approach (Davies and Lerner,

---

[2] See Whitesel for helpful evaluations of the strengths and weaknesses of five approaches to multicultural church, which are described using different terminology.

[3] For a variant of this approach, see Whitesel, pp. 25–7.

pp. 173–7). In some churches this may be on a rotational basis, but 'multicultural inclusion' can also apply to an occasional service.

4 Intercultural Integration

Churches following an *integrated* approach have music teams, often with culturally diverse members, who learn and lead songs from diverse cultures, including the majority culture. Their aim is to 'integrate' the cultures together in worship. Some call this the 'blended' approach (Whitesel, pp. 31–3; Van Opstal, pp. 105–7; Davies and Lerner, pp. 178–80; Black, 2000, pp. 95–7), but 'blended' often refers to combining hymns and contemporary music, while 'integrated worship' applies to a wider diversity including songs of the world church.

5 Intercultural Innovation

In multi-ethnic churches adopting an *innovative* approach, sometimes called 'fusion' (Davis and Lerner, pp. 180–1), musicians from different cultures create and arrange together. They collaborate to compose songs or tailor-make existing songs for their community's people, range of music styles and languages. In some churches this can lead to a worship sound unique to that church. Nikki Lerner describes how, with gifted musical leadership, Bridgeway Community Church in Columbia, Maryland, developed its own 'Bridgeway' sound (Lerner, p. 98). Well-crafted 'fusions' may work but there is a risk that an underlying style will make everything sound the same and distinctive flavours will get lost (like covering food from different cuisines in the same sauce!). So intercultural creative collaborations should bring out those distinctives, offering each to Jesus.

6 Intercultural Illumination

Intercultural *illumination* refers to shining a spotlight on one or two cultures in particular services. Churches doing this give space to specific cultural groups to lead a whole service or event in their own way, with support from the others. The preparation is an intercultural activity where the cultural group takes the initiative to suggest materials and others are involved in helping to make it work for their multi-ethnic setting. Sandra Maria Van Opstal calls this 'collaborative rotation' (p. 107), emphasizing the intercultural collaboration involved. This can happen in regular services or in special events, such as a National Day or Lunar New Year.

Advantages and Disadvantages of Each Approach

The first step is to identify where your church is right now. If it is not one of the above, draw your own diagram depicting your church in relation to how many musical and worship cultures are present in regular services. There are good reasons for each approach. Please note that 'approaches' is a better term than 'models', since none are pre-designed, factory-made models. Each church decides how it will incorporate cultural diversity depending on context. I outline below some benefits and downsides of each approach, with examples.

1 Monocultural Inheritance

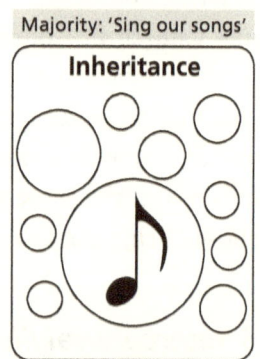

In multi-ethnic churches adopting a monocultural approach, worship leaders select common songs in a widely used language. Here there is uniformity, a kind of unity, but no expression of cultural diversity.

- **Advantages:** monocultural worship can work for national and international gatherings, where a uniformity of music style creates a sense of unity and predictability.

- **Disadvantages:** the music and worship style privileges some cultures but marginalizes others.

Across the world a great number of multi-ethnic churches operate with some variant of the monocultural approach. Larger, well-known churches may see this as their only option. However, pioneers among them may realize that diversifying their musical, linguistic and cultural representation could extend their reach. Experimenting with the intercultural approaches below will help this transition, but we need to pursue this with integrity and consistency, guarding against tokenism. I remember an annual 'international service' in Leeds where a South American man clearly enjoyed the diverse 'vibe'. He came back over the next few Sundays – to the church's usual monocultural worship – and his disappointment was clear.

2 Multi-Congregational Independence

In a multi-congregational church, each group celebrates in its own language and culture – in separate groups. Leaders of the diverse groups may interact (shown by the dashed border) but there is little whole-church unity.

Multi-Congregational Independence
'Sing your songs in your own groups'

Diversity in Groups

- **Advantages:** culture-specific worship avoids the awkwardness of language and cultural differences by creating a 'home from home' community. It is ideal for reaching and discipling certain language groups, especially first-generation immigrants.
- **Disadvantages:** this can exacerbate cultural isolation and drive a wedge between parents and children who more easily identify with the host language and culture; they find their ethnic fellowship less relevant and they more easily drift away from church.

St James's Church of England, Alperton, Northwest London, has long been an example of a multi-congregational model – with good reason. Madeleine Davies of the *Church Times* reports:

> *In the parish of St James', Alperton, in west London, home to a large Gujarati-speaking population, most people were born abroad, and almost half are Hindu. The church has four congregations, including Hindi-speaking and Tamil-speaking ones, who come together regularly to worship. At these services of celebration, multiple languages are used, and translations are available for all. It is an approach in which 'everyone is equally inconvenienced', one of its priests, the Revd Steve Taylor, says.*

I visited this church in February 2024. The vicars, Steve and Ali Taylor, have clearly navigated a path between worship in four separate congregations (the multi-congregational approach) and a more unified celebration (using various intercultural approaches), where all the languages and cultures are present and represented in every part of the Sunday service. They have jointly written a multilingual song. Since the 2020 Covid lockdowns, this church has moved from a monthly combined gathering to a weekly intercultural church service. The primary emphasis has shifted from separate groups to one intercultural community (integration). The church is seeing God at work in many ways and is growing.

3 Multicultural Inclusion

In the 'inclusive' approach, each cultural group is invited to lead the whole church by turn (for example, on a monthly rota or taking different sections of a service). There is visible cultural diversity, fostering unity.

Multicultural
'Sing your songs for us'
Inclusion
culture groups lead songs (in turns)

Invited Diversity

- **Advantages:** each group takes ownership and makes decisions; they feel valued.

- **Disadvantages:** It can lead to 'spectator' worship because the style and language is natural for those leading but may be difficult or unappealing for others. As a result, some 'switch off' or choose not to attend church when the worship style does not suit them.

Two different examples could be helpful to illustrate how this can look.

An East London church operated a rotational model for a while, with four ethnic groupings leading songs once a month. One Sunday when I visited, a Sierra Leonean song leader explained he wanted to diverge from this pattern to include a South Asian song. He explained to me afterwards that some people were staying away on particular Sundays because of the cultural group leading. He wanted to demonstrate that all could be involved in different styles and languages. He had identified a problem in this approach and was instinctively moving towards greater 'integration' of worship cultures (approach #4).

Another church held a large pre-Christmas 'international service' for their forty-or-so ethnicities. City dignitaries were invited and my wife and I thought this might be suitable for a non-Christian international student who had never been to church. However, it was not well thought through. Each cultural grouping took to the stage, sang two songs, enthusiastically inviting everyone to 'join in' with words we had to try to pronounce. After a while, this became an extremely long 'variety show'.

Weaknesses of the 'Multicultural Inclusion' Approach

I should qualify something about this: this latter event in no way invalidates the 'international service' idea. At the same time, it demonstrates the weakness of holding a service like this only occasionally. It is easy to squeeze too much in! It is therefore a good object lesson for multicultural worship: don't introduce so many songs at the same time!

From both examples, we learn that 'multicultural inclusion' appears to be a great approach and very empowering. The biggest downside is that it can result in creating too much cultural distance between the leading groups and others – unless they have enough understanding or guidance about how to introduce their songs to a multi-ethnic congregation. They may be so eager to share something special to them that they build barriers to congregational engagement. What is intuitive to them is not natural to others, and bridges need to be built.

The bridges we need to build are facilitated by adopting the three 'intercultural' approaches suggested below: 'integration', 'innovation' and 'illumination'. Combining two or three of these can result in churches developing a worship culture that fits its congregation. For clarity, let's take them one at a time.

4 Intercultural Integration

To be 'integrated', worship music is chosen from more than one culture in a single service. Here there is tangible diversity and enjoyment of unity through active participation.

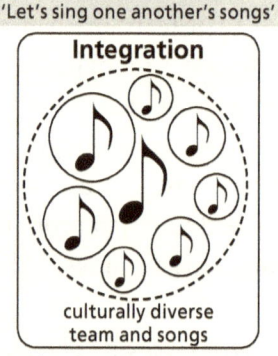

Intercultural
'Let's sing one another's songs'
Integration
culturally diverse team and songs
Sharing in Diversity

- **Advantages:** people see the varied styles as integrated into an experience of worship; worship leaders are learners themselves, so they are more likely to choose songs others can learn; hence the approach encourages participation.
- **Disadvantages:** it requires an intentional openness to other languages and styles, and songs may lose something of their original cultural flavour if they are too mixed with musical elements from the church's core musical style.

Intercultural integration seemed to be the approach of a London church plant. Led by Jessie Tang of Songs2Serve, the worship group led a mix of contemporary Christian songs, some with a slight 'ethnic twist', plus songs from other cultures. The team included many from non-white British or immigrant backgrounds and the worship languages included English, Chinese, Spanish, German, Italian, Farsi, Hindi, Gujarati, Sinhalese and Tamil (Tang, 2020).

This was also the approach we took in the Oldham church. We held regular socials and practice times for the music team, whose membership became increasingly multi-ethnic. The five worship leaders met periodically to reflect on our approach. On two or three Sundays a month, songs were included from the global South (especially Africa and Asia). Individuals assisted with pronunciation and 'dance' movements they knew. Sheka Tarawalie from Sierra Leone occasionally preached and led in song. This approach aimed at 'integrating' people (interculturally) and music (multiculturally).

5 *Intercultural Innovation*

Intercultural innovation occurs when musicians of different cultures collaborate to arrange songs from various cultures or create new material. There is both diversity and unity through a sense of the church developing its own sound.

Creating in Diversity

- **Advantages:** suitable sounds can be created to highlight certain cultures; people identify well with the new songs since they associate them with people in the church.
- **Disadvantages:** it requires gifted and creative musicianship not always present in smaller churches; some cultures may never be featured; culturally distinctive features may be lost in a common sound.

An example of an interculturally innovative worshipping community is Proskuneo Ministries based in Clarkston, Georgia, USA, led by Josh Davies, Jaewoo and Joy Kim and others from a range of language and cultural backgrounds. Among them are songwriters who collaborate to write in various styles and languages. They got together to produce an album called 1 (*ONE*), written by the community on the theme of unity and diversity.

6 *Intercultural Illumination*

In our sixth approach, church leaders, musicians and members of different cultures lead whole events that give special focus to (or 'illuminate') one or two cultures at a time. There is cultural diversity but unity is promoted through support and participation.

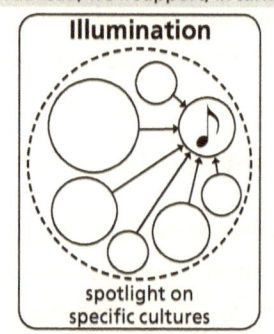

- *Advantages*: each culture is given a chance to take the initiative and involve others with them. They demonstrate not only the songs but the context and atmosphere of their worship culture; culturally distinctive features are not lost.
- *Disadvantages*: it requires sufficient people of each culture to make this work, as well as skill in drawing in those who have never experienced its context. Some cultures may be overlooked if there are too few people or resources.

This is both the most respectful and most challenging model. It is the approach favoured by Sandra Maria Van Opstal. She says: 'Worship retains the authenticity of original style and form. Every community is given an opportunity to lead.' This is important because:

> *Unless we have a community of diverse leaders who can speak into the situation and co-create spaces, we will repeatedly go to our favorite foods, music, decorations and event planning processes. (Van Opstal, p. 80)*

Gathering these distinct voices allows the leading group to express 'deeper cultural values' and therefore gives the greatest ownership and voice to each worship culture. It requires enough people and resources to pull it off and, if done too frequently, can generate learning fatigue. On the other hand, Van Opstal says this can be manageable, if done on a monthly or six-weekly cycle, allowing time for each event to be well prepared.

The Revd Dr Warren Beattie explains how the community at the Discipleship Training Centre in Singapore used this approach in their college life once every three months. He says that factors such as music, language, the use of physical space, dress, food and how people interact are areas to think through. The entire event is shaped by the cultural group, with the support of leaders (2016, pp. 126–8). Van Opstal says:

> *This approach is distinctive in that it is not primarily about collecting songs and components from different traditions and assigning people from those traditions to lead (tokenism), but allowing the traditions of team members to shape the overall community and worship experience. (p. 80)*

The most significant advantage of this is that each culture is given a chance to shine, to be understood on its own terms. It avoids the dangers of cultural appropriation, where others determine how they want to import features of a culture's music, dance or worship. We have also seen that this approach may be too demanding to stand on its own but works well with other methods, as below:

> **Combining the Three Intercultural Approaches**
>
> 1 Worship teams can bring songs together from a mix of cultures (*Integration*).
>
> 2 Musicians can collaborate, create and arrange music across cultures (*Innovation*).
>
> 3 Each culture can be heard on its own terms (*Illumination*).

📍 Plotting a Route Between Current Practice and Your Dream Scenario

Why not pause here to pray, and review the above approaches, comparing them to your situation? Having identified your starting point and hoped-for destination, it could help to plot a route between these two. After all, the writer of Proverbs says: 'In their hearts humans plan their course, but the Lord establishes their steps' (Prov. 16.9). This verse assumes that planning is a positive thing. At the same time it also recognizes that we do not know how things will turn out and, ultimately, God oversees how they do. Therefore people from cultures that value precise planning may need to hold plans lightly and those who value spontaneity may consider setting some plans, however loose. This could involve the following.

Refining Your Vision Statement

If you have already written down your vision statement for intercultural worship, why not take time to refine or add to it, in the light of the six approaches and what these have brought to your attention? What are your strengths and weaknesses?

Identifying Current Strengths and Weaknesses

What are your church's strengths?

Your church's strong points (people, resources and attitudes) will help fulfil this dream. How can you maximize your strengths?

What do you currently lack in your church?

What you lack may look insurmountable, but with God nothing is impossible (Luke 18.27). Your deficiencies may also be people, resources and attitudes, so how can you fill these gaps?

For example, if you lack people who can play instruments, different approaches can be taken.

If You Have no one to Play Instruments

- Find musicians who can train church people in music, either for free or find funds for this.
- Until musicians are available, use musical video resources.
- Experiment with other arts and non-musical intercultural worship.
- Invite people to pray and read the Bible in their languages.
- Encourage testimonies, stories of faith.
- Use worship poetry from across the world.

Pray about Your First Two or Three Steps

Having done all the above, start to consider some first steps to pray about.

AN INTERCULTURAL WORSHIP HANDBOOK

Possible First Steps

1 If a church member knows suitable songs from their background, why not suggest they meet up with church musicians to teach these songs?

2 If your music team cannot lead this song, perhaps the individual could sing it in a small group, a service when you pray for their people, or during the offering?

3 If the same person is not confident to sing publicly, could a video of the song be played at some point, perhaps with that person reading Bible verses or praying for their country?

4 If no such song materials are available, you could consider prayer and Bible verses that help highlight the needs of people in this person's 'home' country.

In later chapters, we will come to practical ways to pursue intercultural worship. First, however, we will consider the importance of areas that many people do not realize are so important for the effectiveness of worship: the vital role of musical diversity, the impact of 'heart music' and how diverse worship cultures can work together.

 Questions to Ponder

1 In one sentence, how would you express your primary goal for intercultural worship?
2 Of the six common approaches to culture in worship, what is your current starting point?
3 What dream destination do you have a vision to work towards?
4 What first steps could you take to move towards this?

5

Singing:
Musical Diversity in Worship

Our worship must be multicultural, not simply because our society is multicultural, but because the future from which God is calling us is multicultural ... Not just so that those from other cultures may feel at home among us but also so that we may feel at home in God's future. (Adeney, p. 281, quoting Justo González)

This chapter gives attention to musical and linguistic diversity in song. Perhaps more obviously than anything else, music has the potential to demonstrate what being intercultural looks, sounds and feels like. First we look at how the early church used music and song. Second we find inspiration from developments in the wider musical culture around us. After that I address some common causes for resistance to musical diversity. Finally I present seven broader reasons to embrace worship diversity. Chapter 6 ('Understanding: The Impact of Heart Music') will then focus on another major reason for musical diversity.

Evidence for Diversity of Song Style in New Testament Worship

The Apostle Paul encourages believers in the cosmopolitan church in Ephesus to 'be filled with the Spirit ... and make music from your heart to the Lord' (Eph. 5.18–19). What could this music have sounded like? A manuscript with musical notation survives, possibly from the third century (Hilton, 'The Oxyrhynchus Hymn'), and some musicians and researchers have attempted to recover traces of the music in Israel around the time of Jesus, which may help us to imagine influences on early Christian song (see SAVAE). What we can propose, however, is that Christian worship reflected the diversity of the first believers and the variety of their backgrounds,.

Context

In 1 Corinthians 14.26, Paul described the sharing of contributions by all the gathered worshippers:

> *What then shall we say, brothers and sisters? When you come together, each of you has a hymn, or a word of instruction, a revelation, a tongue or an interpretation. Everything must be done so that the church may be built up.*

Song

First, the New Testament depicts song as part of Christian worship along with a shared meal in the homes of believers (1 Cor. 11—15; Mark 14.26; Acts 2.46a; 12.12; 16.40; Rom. 16.5; 1 Cor. 16.19; Col. 4.15). Researchers have been able to build up a picture of the role of song in these assemblies (McKinnon; Alikin, pp. 211–53; Page). An older view held that Christian song was influenced by music in the temple or synagogue. Of course, Jewish liturgical influences on Christian worship were strongly present from the outset but some scholars assert that the scriptures were not sung in synagogues until later (Alikin, p. 215), while temple music was specialist and connected to the sacrificial system. However, it was common in the Greek and Roman world for songs to be sung after evening meals (social gatherings called *symposia*), including in Jewish homes, as was done after the Last Supper (Mark 14.26). It was therefore mainly in homes that Christian song initially developed, when they gathered to worship and celebrate the 'breaking of bread' (Acts 2.42, 46; 1 Cor. 11.17–34). Valeriy Alikin paints this picture:

> *During their assemblies the early Christians sang psalms, odes and hymns. They did so in conformity with the singing at symposia in the Graeco-Roman world. The singing could be accompanied by the music of stringed instruments such as lyre, cithara or harp.*[1] *During their gatherings, the early Christians also prayed. (p. 215)*

James McKinnon says: 'the New Testament ... creates an unmistakable general impression of enthusiasm for sacred song', alongside instruction and fellowship. Scholars cite New Testament passages and other texts from the first three centuries that recount singing in worship as a regular feature of early church worship (Alikin, pp. 211–27; McKinnon, pp. 1–6).

Languages

Second, those who offered a contribution to worship would have spoken or sung with their own accent. The whole area was a linguistic melting pot, where the 'principal languages of early Christian music were Greek, Latin and Syriac' (Syriac was Aramaic, the language of Jesus), with Greek quickly becoming the dominant Christian language in the areas of Paul's ministry (McKinnon, p. 1). In addition, Paul and Luke mention the 'Barbarians'[2] (their speech was not Greek and to Greeks sounded unintelligible, like 'bar-bar'), and 'Scythians' (Col. 3.11), the most feared of 'barbarian' ethnic groups (Martin,

---

1 Alikin's terms are confusing and appear to refer to the same instrument type. This is the *kithara* (the Greek word referenced in 1 Cor. 14.7; Rev. 5.8; 14.2; 15.2; 18.22), a lyre, often confusingly translated as a 'harp' in earlier English translations. It is related to the *kinnor* played by David (in Hebrew). See Montagu, pp. 125–6.

2 'Barbaros': Acts 28.2, 4; Rom. 1.14; 14.11; 1 Cor. 14.11; Col. 3.11. The Greek word is sometimes translated into English as 'non-Greek', 'native', 'foreigner', 'barbarous'.

1978, p. 108).³ The overall scene is of widely used written and trading languages as well as regional dialects and tribal languages. At the same time, Paul encourages Christians to speak with understanding when they come together.

Music

Third, Christians who offered their songs in the assemblies would have drawn from musical styles familiar to them. We should note that Christian song could have been mostly vocal, without instruments, giving focus to the message (Col. 3.16). This is the overriding evidence in the available accounts. Although Paul mentions instruments in 1 Corinthians 14.7–8 in a section about order in public worship, it is used simply as an illustration not an instruction. However, many early church writers condemned the use of instruments (McKinnon, pp. 13–14; James-Griffiths) because of their associations with idol worship and immoral practices. Some scholars point out that this rejection may not have been universally applied, especially in the case of the *kithara* lyre (Alikin, p. 227), the 'most respected of all instruments' (Montagu, p. 125). However, even if the lyre was an exception, the general impression is of unaccompanied song in Christian gatherings. Furthermore, while some songs could have been sung by the whole assembly, many would have been presented solo (1 Cor. 14.26; Eph. 5.19; Col. 3.16; James 5.13). The whole congregation could sometimes join in with an acclamation, such as 'Amen', 'Alleluia', 'Maranatha' or a doxology (McKinnon, p. 4). Of relevance to us, each person's distinct voice had an opportunity to be heard – their insights, language and song style. As we have seen, such mutual listening and sharing is a key feature of intercultural worship.

---

3 Regarded as 'little better than wild beasts'; Josephus, *Contra Apionem* ii.269, cited by Martin, 1978, p. 108.

Psalms, Hymns and Spiritual Songs

Fourth, in certain passages we discern diversity of music. Paul twice uses a threefold description of church songs. In Ephesians 5.18–20 he says:

> *be filled with the Spirit, speaking to one another with psalms, hymns, and songs from the Spirit. Sing and make music from your heart to the Lord, always giving thanks to God the Father for everything, in the name of our Lord Jesus Christ.*

And similarly in Colossians 3.16:

> *Let the message of Christ dwell among you richly as you teach and admonish one another with all wisdom through psalms, hymns, and songs from the Spirit, singing to God with gratitude in your hearts.*

It is not clear whether 'psalms, hymns, and songs from the Spirit' refers to three distinct forms or if it was shorthand for 'all types of song'. Either way, there is indication here of musical diversity. In his comments on Colossians 3.16, the worship theologian Ron Man muses that 'in the Colossian church Paul encouraged the inclusion of musical expressions indigenous to the various groups he refers to in v. 11' (p. 253). Likewise, Constance Cherry suggests that the multicultural context of pluralistic cities like Ephesus and Colossae 'would have fostered a breadth of song as the early church grew in diversity' (pp. 157–8).

The Greek words for 'psalms, hymns, and songs from the Spirit' overlap in meaning, but what can we deduce about musical style? First, there was Jewish influence. The early church sang, or recited, Old Testament psalms whose poetic and musical styles came from a Jewish heritage. There are other texts that also reflect this Jewish background, such as those attributed to Mary and Zechariah, later known as 'canticles', and by their Latin names the *Magnificat* (Luke 1.46–55) and the *Benedictus* (Luke 1.68–79), although it is uncertain how soon these came to be used as songs (McKinnon, p. 4). Next, there was undoubtedly Greek influence. While 'hymn' can refer to Hebrew-style biblical psalms, such as Mark 14.26 (possibly Psalms 115–18; Hendriksen, p. 576), it can also mean 'an ecstatically inspired hymn of thanksgiving' (Martin, 1978, p. 115) or newly composed Christian hymns, hints of which may be found in New Testament passages (Martin, 1964, pp. 47–52; Bartels, p. 674).[4] In reality, because Greek culture was all-pervasive, Cherry says that 'hymnic forms common to Greek society would have been employed to create songs to sing to Christ as God' (p. 158).

Lastly, what about 'spiritual songs'? Ralph Martin sees these as 'snatches of spontaneous praise' (1964, p. 47) or as a musical composition (1974, p. 115). Cherry notes that 'there is widespread consensus that they arose spontaneously from within the worshipping community' (p. 158). Such songs are extremely likely to have reflected melodic patterns and rhythms that each singer instinctively knew from his or her upbringing, including, most naturally, folk traditions. Alec Robertson considered this probable:

At the assemblies, as the words of St Paul ... suggest, there was room for free improvisation as the spirit moved this or that person to testify; and with the influx of Gentiles foreign to Jewish tradition and laws, one may well believe that these converts sometimes used folks-songs familiar to them for their inspired utterances. (p. 141)

This overview illustrates that, at the very least, music in the early churches drew on Jewish, Greek and regional song forms. So however imperfectly we understand worship in early Christianity, there was undoubtedly linguistic, cultural and musical diversity. This raises the question: If singing in the early church was diverse, what is worship in our churches like? Are the voices of people from diverse cultures being heard in our churches? God is surely worthy that we should bring to

---

4 Including the following passages, although scholars are unclear whether these were originally songs or heightened writing: Rom. 3.24–26; Eph. 5.14; Phil. 2.6–11; Col. 1.15–20; 1 Tim 3.16.

him praise that reflects the breadth of human creativity. Inspiration for this is not only drawn from diversity in the early church, hazily glimpsed from scant sources, but also from its abundance in the world of music around us today.

A Flourishing of Musical Diversity in the World Around Us

In our increasingly interconnected world, human diversity is being celebrated. Musicians engage in intercultural collaborations, seeking connections and ways to combine musical influences, often with stimulating results. These musicians discover a new kind of synergy observable in almost all genres of music, from Asian, African and European folk and classical traditions to the multiple genres of popular music. The Benin-born singer Angélique Kidjo collaborates with artists, cross-pollinating 'West African traditions … with elements of R&B, funk and jazz, as well as influences from Europe and Latin America' (Kidjo, 2024). The Silk Road Ensemble, founded by the cellist Yo-Yo Ma, 'creates music that engages difference, sparking radical cultural collaboration and passion-driven learning for a more hopeful and inclusive world … When we create music together, we listen to our differences, connecting and creating meaning from them' (Silkroad).

Postures to Adopt: Listening, Connecting, Creating and Celebrating Diversity

This vision for a 'more inclusive world' is inspiring for intercultural worship. We can learn from their attitude:

> *When we create music together, we listen to our differences, connecting and creating meaning from them. (Silkroad)*

They embody postures of 'listening', 'connecting' and 'creating'. Likewise, when believers listen to one another before God, they allow space for the Holy Spirit to connect hearts together and, from that interconnectivity, to create something new and beautiful. Further, Angélique Kidjo is dedicated to 'celebrating human diversity'. Her perspective is captured in an interview with *Songlines* magazine:

> we cannot live without each other … We need each other … We all have the same needs. Pain has no colour. Tears [have] no colour. I'll continue celebrating our human diversity till my last breath. Because if we lose that diversity, we lose our humanity. (Kidjo, 2023, p. 35)

These examples provide a broader backdrop for encouraging musical diversity in worship. Listening, connecting, creating and celebrating human diversity can start very simply, by learning a song from a fellow worshipper. We go into more detail later but before that, let's revisit the matter of resistance to diversity.

Most Obstacles to Musical Diversity Can be Overcome

In Chapter 3, we focused on some pastoral and practical objections to musical diversity. Now we address some deeper reasons for resistance. It is my firm belief that, for churches who hold an intercultural vision, most objections can be overcome with a commitment to loving our neighbour as ourselves. Many believers are persuaded from the scriptures of the general *idea* of intercultural worship but – when it comes to actual *practice* – resistance can surface even with slight changes in musical style. This is nothing new and is true of *any* musical style. In other words, if church leaders and musicians introduce it well, musical diversity worship can distance fewer people than it attracts, because of its wider appeal. This is how the legendary evangelist Billy Graham wisely replied to someone unhappy with 'new music' in church:

Instead of complaining to your pastor (or anyone else), I urge you to ask God to help you be grateful for all music that points us to God, new or old. No, you may not like some of it, but others do, and God can use it in their lives to encourage them and bring them closer to Christ. Remember: The old hymns you like were once new, and someone probably didn't like them, either! (Graham)

This comment is relevant for multi-ethnic congregations since it points to our hearts, not just to musical style: our reactions can mask underlying attitudes. For multi-ethnic congregations, two of the harder hurdles are racial bias and individualism.

Racial Bias

The first nut to crack is racial bias. Others have far greater expertise in this area than me and I recommend gaining wise advice from such people before tackling this in a local church. You can draw counsel from webinars, consultations, books (such as Roach and Birdsall; Lindsay; Hylton) and the like. It is a highly sensitive issue. Some have been profoundly wounded by racist abuse. Others are offended that others see prejudice in them. The fact is we all have blind spots. For this reason, leaders need to approach this with a combination of love and clarity. Hopefully, they will be able to address the topic in a non-confrontational manner, in a variety of contexts (publicly, in small groups and privately), as well as listen to a range of voices and discuss appropriate ways forward for the church. Leaders may also need to examine their own hearts. For musical matters, worship leaders could feel especially vulnerable.

The fundamental question could be: 'Is there an unconscious attitude that privileges worship from our majority group?' Digging deeper, does this suggest a subconscious assumption that just one culture, one musical style, one church tradition (that is, 'mine') can *adequately* represent God's praise? This begins to look very much like cultural pride. If so, soul-searching and repentance will be needed:

this is a discipleship issue before it is a worship issue – addressing heart attitudes. Once we start to address this, we can look for ways to move forward where we commit to learning to 'value others above yourselves … looking … to the interests of others' (Phil. 2.3–4) – including their worship aspirations. This process cannot be rushed. It takes time, but in two local churches I have been a part of, I have seen mindsets change and people valuing the growing intercultural dimensions of worship.

In one church, leaders addressed this issue head-on by gathering groups of people from varied backgrounds over time to discuss racial bias, casting a vision for an intercultural church and bringing biblical teaching to the whole church about how to build cross-cultural relationships. The process continues in conversations and strategies to promote diversity in church life.

Individualism

A second nut to crack is individualism. This is a spiritual and cultural stronghold in western societies. To our shame, we all too easily bring a 'me-centred' mentality into worship gatherings, looking for what 'I' can get out of it. In its extreme form, the 'success' of a time of worship is assessed by looking inward to our response to the music and songs. It places an unreasonable burden on musicians if our experience is tied almost exclusively to how well they carry us along emotionally. By contrast, worship in the New Testament was far less about the music; it was more about the message (Col. 3.16). Rather, worship is about a transformation that takes place in us week-by-week as we gather with others to worship Jesus, sing to God and one another, hear his words and respond in various ways, being equipped once again for our life as lights in the world. Of course, God is truly interested in us *feeling* close to him (Ps. 27.4), but we also know he is more interested in our heart *transformation*, becoming more like Christ (Rom. 12). Indeed, our meeting with Christ need not be hindered by others. Instead, it is often through others that we encounter Christ. Our unity with each other, despite or because of our human failings, is a place of abundant blessing (Ps. 133). In short, true intercultural worship is not a joy-killer. It is a joy-giver – giving more than it demands. I have seen this time and time again.

Introducing Intercultural Worship

Whether resistance comes from uncertainty about how to do intercultural worship or deeper issues of racial bias, individualistic attitudes or something else, it is always good to remember that any change necessarily takes time, and introducing culturally diverse songs becomes easier when two golden principles are observed.

Two Golden Principles

1. Let love be the basis (loving neighbour as oneself).
2. Take time and make the process easy for people.

Seven More Reasons for Diversity in Worship

We now look at seven 'big' reasons for cultural diversity in worship. This section is intended to further help leaders graciously guide the church towards this end.

1 God is Glorified by Cultural Diversity in Worship

John Piper aptly says, 'the beauty and power of praise that will come to the Lord from the diversity of the nations are greater than the beauty and power that would come to him if the chorus of the redeemed were culturally uniform' (1993, p. 225).

This first reason puts the emphasis on how our worship reflects the God we serve. While this may appear rather theoretical, it is fundamentally practical. It asks: 'What do our worship practices tell others about the nature of our God?' It may do many things well but in what ways does it demonstrate God's creativity, his love of diversity and his desire that all the nations and tribes should be represented? In today's churches, musical diversity is usually the most visible expression of this.

2 Culturally Diverse Worship Values Others – And This Glorifies God

> *Accept one another, then, just as Christ accepted you, in order to bring praise to God. (Rom. 15.7)*

Paul says that the very act of accepting one another *is* worship – it brings God praise! By contrast, self-absorbed singing can be dangerous, especially if it falls into the subtle unconscious trap of 'worshipping worship'. Jesus summarized the two most important commands as 'love God' and 'love your neighbour' (Mark 12.29–31). We naturally relate the first to worship but what about 'loving our neighbour' in worship? In multi-ethnic churches our 'neighbour' includes the culturally other person, as in Jesus' parable about this (the Samaritan in Luke 10.25–37). Does this not mean that we give space to all church members, even if we lay aside our personal preferences for a song or two? The writer of Hebrews speaks of offering God a 'sacrifice of praise' when we do good to others:

> *Through Jesus, therefore, let us continually offer to God a sacrifice of praise – the fruit of lips that openly profess his name. And do not forget to do good and to share with others, for with such sacrifices God is pleased. (Heb. 13.15–16)*

We could say that a willingness to consider others before ourselves *becomes* an offering pleasing to God. This second reason, then, is pastoral and addresses our social awareness. It is also good for our discipleship. It challenges any selfishness in our approach to corporate worship (2 Sam. 24.24). Intercultural musical diversity may initially cost us a little, but in time it begins to bless us in unexpected ways too (Acts 20.35).

3 Intercultural Worship Challenges Pride

Almost all of us have cultural pride, including the way we do things in church. 'Our way of doing things here' can easily become an idol – raising barriers to mutual understanding. Fortunately, we have an antidote: intercultural worship helps put our own ethnic pride in its place, because we begin to see our culture as one among many (James 4.6; 1 Pet. 5.5). This can sometimes be a powerfully life-changing experience. Over some weeks our band taught songs to a Zimbabwean-majority church in Leeds, including a Turkish song with English translation. There was a Hungarian present, a strong Christian, whose national history resulted in a shared hatred of Turks. The song musically melted her heart and she realized that she too had imbibed this prejudice – until that moment. God was powerfully clearing away long-established, inherited cultural barriers through song. Wow!

This third reason similarly shows that intercultural worship is countercultural and helps our discipleship. It challenges our hidden values. If we feel uncomfortable in culturally diverse worship, this can be a very sacred place: the Holy Spirit could be at work! In this way, sensitively led intercultural worship can help us to not conform to our culture but to be transformed by the renewing of our mind (Rom. 12.2).

4 Intercultural Worship Enriches Our Vision

Piper also says: 'There is a greater power and depth to the praise that comes to God from unity in diversity than simply from uniformity' (1998).

In 2020, one song circulated the world with notable effect. It was 'The Blessing' song by Elevation Worship. It could simply have been another song that ended up being sung and played in the same way in different translations. What was remarkable was that within a very short time, this became an icon of cultural identity. Several groups rearranged it to fit their cultural singing style, instrumentation, harmonization, rhythms, dress and visual presentation. This included a Ugandan a cappella choral version, a symphonic version, an Indian version in 31 languages, a Japanese version with traditional instruments and a Greater Middle East version in several languages. Seeing such eagerness to identify as the one global church of Jesus opened more people's eyes to the presence of the church in other nations – many of whom wanted to express oneness with the world church but, rightly, on their own cultural terms. These 'contextualized' adaptations demonstrated a unity but also a desire for the beauty of cultural distinctives to be seen and heard.

In intercultural worship we get a bigger vision of God and of the possibilities in worship. This lifts our eyes to hear the voices of churches in other countries and regions, to pray for them and to offer our praise with them. This leads us to a fifth big reason.

5 Intercultural Worship Reveals More About God and Worship

Culturally diverse worship takes us on a journey into new understandings about our faith. To take a few examples:

From the worship of Africans I know, I have learned how God loves community and movement in worship. Indeed, some question whether there could be hidden sin in our lives if we are not free enough to dance (King, 2018, p. 184)! Likewise, songs that set the exact words of scripture to song help us remember them and they build faith through repetition. For example, 'Once you have spoken' by the British Nigerian worship leader Muyiwa Olarewaju sets verses almost exactly from Psalm 62.

From Persian believers I gain a deep sense of the Holy Spirit in song, that the poetry of the words is a gift and that Christ has set the worshippers free, expressed in tears or dance, through his sacrifice on the cross (Kalameh, 2025b; Elam TV; Arts Release, 2018). I have also seen non-Persians moved to tears through these songs.

From Indian Christian devotional songs (*Yeshu Bhajans*) sung in a call-and-response format, I experience an intimacy of worship that is also communal. Songs like 'Amrit Vani' are meditative and joyous, often dwelling on the names of Jesus or a gospel truth (Aradhna, 2015).

This fifth reason demonstrates that intercultural worship deepens our worship experience in ways that no single culture can. Musical diversity on its own cannot do this, but God's Spirit can take hold of this greater palette of worship forms to speak into my heart and mind to expand my heart and vision.

6 Intercultural Worship Impacts the World Around Us

Let us not underestimate the power of a worshipping multicultural church to impact the wider community. In Oldham, people began to take notice of the love, welcome and positive effects of our church's diversity. The local newspaper, the *Oldham Evening Chronicle* ('The Chron'), ran a full article on the multicultural nature of our church. They counted eleven different countries, warmly describing it as a 'Mini United Nations'. They related the stories of several immigrants in our church and quoted Osman, from Sierra Leone, saying that the church, 'was not multi-ethnic when I came but now it is diverse, and I know diversity is part of God's will'. They rounded off with Maria Theresa, a Filipina nurse, asserting, 'I will continue coming. I enjoy their style of service, the diversity and friendliness' (Barker, p. 8).

This sixth big reason points to God's broader mission in the world – to the fact that intercultural churches can be a force for societal culture-change where such worship challenges culture and at the same time demonstrates refreshing ways of living in profound unity amid significant diversity.

7 Intercultural Worship Breathes Evangelistic Potential

On the day of Pentecost, believers praised God in multiple languages through the gift of the Spirit – with outstanding evangelistic results. Bystanders were astounded as they heard the disciples declare God's wonders in their languages. This opened their hearts to the message. Luke narrates the scene in Acts 2.8–12:

> *'Then how is it that each of us hears them in our native language? Parthians, Medes and Elamites; residents of Mesopotamia, Judea and Cappadocia, Pontus and Asia, Phrygia and Pamphylia, Egypt and the parts of Libya near Cyrene; visitors from Rome (both Jews and converts to Judaism); Cretans and Arabs – we hear them declaring the wonders of God in our own tongues!' Amazed and perplexed, they asked one another, 'What does this mean?'*

I have noticed how the faces of non-English speakers light up when worship teams choose a song in their language. Sometimes it is the first Christian song they have ever heard in their mother tongue. It can have a profound impact. Rob Baker and I taught the Hindi-language song 'Amrit Vani' at a seminar in a conference attended by a Nigerian pastor. The following year she related her story. After learning the song she encountered a dejected Muslim man in a London market and sang this song to him. Touching his heart through song led to him attending church, putting his faith in Jesus, joining the church and marrying a Christian woman. Hearing this song in his language was the springboard.

This seventh reason is also about God's mission in the world but shows how God touches individuals, bringing some to accept Christ as their Lord. As we have seen, this communicates especially when the language is their native language and the music is a style they identify with.

These seven big reasons speak of the benefits of musical diversity in Christian worship. Let us now turn to the importance of musical style for individuals – their 'heart music'.

 Questions to Ponder

1. How does worship in the early church encourage musical diversity in our day?
2. What points of resistance to musical diversity do you face in your own heart or church?
3. How can resistance to musical diversity be addressed in your setting?
4. Of the seven big reasons for culturally diverse worship, which ones apply most to your setting?

6

Understanding: The Impact of Heart Music

This chapter will go into some depth about 'heart music' and introduce a sample heart-music survey, a tool that can be used to help the process of listening, which then assists the route to intercultural worship.

People Respond Differently to the Same Music

Some people imagine that everybody responds to the same music in the same way. This is simply not the case. Music is a universal *phenomenon* but not a universal *language* (Harris, 2013, pp. 82–9). This realization may come as a surprise. The phrase 'music is a universal language' has been taken much too literally because there is not just *one* language of music in the world but *many*. We cannot expect to understand the emotional meaning of music, let alone the words, from a culture in which we have no background. However, people often think they can.

For example, I hear people comment that a certain song from another country sounds 'sad, or dark'. Their reaction is subjective and based on their own musical experience – what they have learned is 'sad' or 'dark'. Music we call 'western' uses certain scales ('diatonic'), notes tuned in a certain way ('tempered') and note combinations ('harmonies') that have developed in Europe only over the last four centuries. Typically, music in a minor key is associated with 'sadness'. This is taught through repeated exposure. However, Middle Eastern or Asian tunes that sound 'minor' are not always sad. They are simply

UNDERSTANDING

based on different musical grammars, called *maqāms, dastgāhs, rāgas* or modes, depending on the region[1], and convey different emotions. In fact many beautiful worship songs composed in Middle Eastern cultures are in so-called 'minor' keys. Even a modern-sounding song with harmonies, played on 'western'-style instruments, may be 'minor' in European terms, but is not sad. It just draws on the musical aesthetic from that culture.

A personal example of another musical language may help. After I started listening to North Indian classical instrumentalists (such as Ravi and Anoushka Shankar, Amjad Ali Khan and Kala Ramnath), I went to some performances. On one occasion I was surprised that the audience started clapping in the *middle* of a performance. What I did not know then was that the preceding section of music built up listeners' expectations to hear a kind of resolution through relatively long cycles of rhythm and melodic improvisation that combined in impressive, virtuosic and beautiful ways and landed on the first beat of the cycle that some members of the audience were counting using hand gestures. While I loved the sound and dexterity of the performance, I did not know how to *understand* it.

At the same time, we can grow in our openness to (and understanding of) other musical styles. As we saw earlier, diversifying our range of music has huge potential. O'Neil Dennis, chief editor of the national UK Christian Chart AStepFWD, prophetically suggests that introducing musical variety is one way of fostering real, generation-shaping change. In the book *The [Im]possible Dream*, he says:

> *Our musical tastes have been shaped by the environment we grew up in. Facilitating and encouraging greater tolerance of differing musical styles and genres will create a better legacy for those coming behind us who will live in an even more diverse human landscape. (Clifford and Adedeji, p. 108)*

---

[1] These terms refer to musical features, including what western music calls 'scales', and a complex of rules for composition and improvisation that make up music systems in the Middle Eastern (*maqām, makam*), Persian (*dastgāh*), South Asian (*rāga*) and East Asian worlds (various forms of pentatonic 'modes'). For more, see Miller and Shahriari, chs 5—8.

What is Heart Music?

The notion of heart music explains why we seek out or respond to some types of music more than others. Understanding this can be illuminating and liberating. Let's look at a definition of heart music by Joy Kim:

> *Heart music means the music that penetrates a person's heart, that reflects a person's identity and culture, that touches one's deep thoughts and emotions. It is considered the music that helps people connect with God and with the world around them. (p. 44)*

Effects of Music on Our Bodies, Brains and Emotions

At the root of this concept is the awareness that music evokes *particular* memories and emotions in us, depending on our exposure to music from our earliest days. For this reason, music therapists seek to discover the music and sounds that help clients cope with mental health issues. For example, the ethnomusicologist and former music therapist Mary E. Saurman scientifically measured her clients' blood pressure and heart rate to assess their responses to a range of musical examples. She reported:

> *The results were amazing, and consistent. Whenever someone heard a familiar song or song style which was from their generational vantage point, their blood pressure and heart rate would be within the normal range … When the music presented was unfamiliar, greatly contrasted with their preferred music, or was associated with a negative memory, the individual's heart rate and blood pressure would increase considerably, sometimes to a very high degree. (1995, pp. 1–2)*

Reflecting on this later, she wrote:

> *We found a pattern: The music that people listened to, usually between 16 and 18 years of age, became the music they enjoyed, became the music they preferred, became the music they found relaxing and heart-familiar, which produced a physical relaxation response. (Saurman, 2010)*

From neuroscientists we learn that music releases hormones such as dopamine, serotonin, oxytocin and prolactin into the brain, depending on the selection of music and the context of experiencing it. These then affect our mood, blood pressure, heart rate and body's immune system. Daniel J. Levitin explains that music works in this way because, from the womb, babies start to associate sounds they hear with certain emotions. He says our brains establish emotional connections to music. These develop in particular ways during adolescence, becoming relatively fixed by early adulthood and forming the foundation for our responses to music through the rest of life. Levitin says:

> *There doesn't seem to be a cutoff point for acquiring new tastes in music, but most people have formed their tastes by the age of eighteen or twenty. (p. 232)*

Importance of Heart Music in Worship

In other words, these emotional responses are culturally learned and were formed in the environments we grew up in. They are highly personalized and deeply instinctive; they create instant reactions nanoseconds before our minds start to process them. They affect us for life. This has massive implications for music in church. Four repercussions are worth mentioning.

> ### Four Considerations about Heart Music
>
> 1 Our heart music is unique and may be related to our ethnic cultures – or not.
>
> 2 Our heart music preferences may unconsciously prejudice us against someone else's worship.
>
> 3 Our heart music can be somewhat fluid because music is never isolated from our context. As a result, certain musics are associated in our brains with particular people, emotions, memories and social settings and can develop over time, even if they relate in some way to the time of our musical formation.
>
> 4 To 'love our neighbour as ourselves' in worship means to 'look to the interests of others' (Mark 12.31; Phil. 2.4), musically.

To illustrate the above, let me tell you my heart-music experience. My emotional responses to music are deeply rooted in my personal musical background but they are equally shaped by my social environment. There is a definite fluidity about my heart-music responses, influenced by my emotions, context and the role of the music is playing (such as entertainment, dance, therapy, worship or education). My heart music has also developed over my lifetime, not simply in childhood and adolescence. It has a strong basis in western classical, choral, early music, avant-garde, folk and worship music. All of these laid the foundations, preparing me for a broadening of musical preferences. For example, I came to non-western music after my earlier musical formation. I was surprisingly, but instinctively, drawn to Indian classical instrumental music and then to Tibetan folk, secular and Christian music – because of my close professional involvement with it. Later this expanded to other non-western musics. My early formation wired my musical brain but prepared me for this expansion. Worshipping with Christ's followers in other cultural settings has given me a love for non-western worship. This expansion of our personal heart music is not only my experience – it is probably part of the journey of any church that develops an inclusive worship culture.

Understanding the importance of heart music can be liberating and transformative. John loved worship music from the 1970s. However, he had an inbuilt, negative reaction to some contemporary worship songs we sang in the 1990s and 2000s. He invited me to his small group, where I mentioned heart music in connection with my overseas fieldwork. John later reported that that completely changed his attitudes to church worship. Instead of fighting his personal reactions he started to rejoice in other people's delight. This illustrates the other-centred approach to worship that can result when we truly understand the effects of heart music. In intercultural worship, then, we learn to take account of how musical choices help or hinder others.

Positive Results of Heart Music

In the section above we have learned that a person's heart music has a very positive effect on them emotionally and spiritually. This is very clear to see in worship and it is usually easy to relate to in terms of our own experiences.

1 The Calming Effects

A person's heart music is much more likely to calm them and make them ready to receive a touch from God, as when King Saul was troubled by a harmful spirit. There were spiritual, mental and emotional causes. In 1 Samuel 16 we are told that his courtiers sent for someone who could play the lyre, a plucked stringed instrument called the *kinnor*. The shepherd boy David was summoned and the effects of this music on Saul were profound:

> *And whenever the harmful spirit from God was upon Saul, David took the lyre and played it with his hand. So Saul was refreshed and was well, and the harmful spirit departed from him. (1 Sam. 16.23 ESV)*

The king's advisors understood the therapeutic potential of the right kind of music. Was Saul's response simply the effect of the Holy Spirit's presence on David? This is the main interpretation I deduce from the passage. At the same time, music therapists might ask, if David had chosen to play the *wrong* kind of music, music that did not appeal to Saul, would this have had the same effect? We cannot say for sure but from all that we learn from music psychology, it was *also* the effect of David's sensitive and culturally appropriate music that changed Saul's mood, enabled by the Holy Spirit.

This is exactly the effect of heart music on people in worship. If a certain instrument, rhythm, sound or volume level is off-putting to a worshipper it can raise barriers to worship. At the same time, if the music resonates with their heart music, it can release them to worship. It is my experience; it may also be yours. This is an important reason for musical diversity in order to include more people.

2 The Inspiring Effects

We are also more likely to pay attention to God's word if the music is helpful. In 2 Kings, Elisha felt the need of a musician. A player of a stringed instrument (probably a *kinnor*; Montagu, p. 60) is summoned to help Elisha bring God's word into an awkward situation of international tension. The effect of the music was immediate:

> *And when the musician played, the hand of the* Lord *came upon him. And he said, 'Thus says the* Lord *...' (2 Kings 3.15–16* esv*)*

This is another example of the right kind of music, Elisha's culturally familiar music. When he heard it, Elisha became more ready to receive the inspired word of God. You too may have found that music helps open you to God's word and, conversely, the wrong type of music can be distracting or disturbing. It is not that God cannot speak with other types of music. It is rather that music can also erect barriers.

3 The Liberating Effects

Singing the right music can be liberating and plays an often unrecognized role in worship. The purpose of worship music is that, during the service, all should be able to 'sing and make music from [the] heart to the Lord' (Eph. 5.18–20). Here we should note that if we follow Paul's directive to 'be filled with the Spirit' we can *learn* to worship God with songs that are not our heart music. Wonderfully, the Holy Spirit enables us. Having said this, let us do all we can to open musical pathways for people rather than build roadblocks!

4 The Evangelistic Potential

People's own musical forms open them more easily to the message of Jesus. One notable example is from India. The rock musician Chris Hale learned the *sitar* and sang Christian devotional songs in North Indian villages. Frank Fortunato writes how they used the devotional heart music loved by millions of Hindus but set to biblical themes and lyrics:

> *By offering the villagers the sounds that they grew up with, but invested with the Truth of the Creator of the universe, the Holy Spirit had the opportunity to move a sincere, devout follower of religious philosophical Hindu thought to a Biblical understanding of Jesus, Lord and Savior. Such truth was not just for the rural, lower-caste Hindu but the urban upper-class Hindu as well ... As seeds of the Christian message were planted ... and eventually these Hindus decided to follow Christ. Two churches were eventually started.* (Fortunato)

The same is true of multi-ethnic worship, as we saw in the example of the Nigerian pastor who sang a Hindi song to a Muslim man in a London market. Such people feel embraced by the love of God through their heart music and language.

Arguments Against Heart Music

It would be good to recognize that there are counterarguments to the necessity of heart music in worship.

First, some consider heart music too simplistic a concept that belongs better to distinct monocultures, each with its own language and 'indigenous' musical culture (Kim, pp. 39–49). In ethnodoxology (the study of how different ethnic groups worship God), heart music came to prominence in these homogenous contexts (Avery). Ethnodoxologists saw it as analogous to 'heart language'. Now we live in a heterogenous world where people usually have a range of heart musics. Further, ethnodoxologists focus on all the arts of a community, not just music, preferring to express similar ideas with more nuanced phrases. All this is true, but it risks underplaying the neuroscience that underscores the heart music concept: that musical preferences develop in our brains and emotions during our formative years, regardless of whether our upbringing is in a homogenous tribe or a diasporic/bicultural context, in multiple countries or a globalized setting. Those raised in multiple cultures (including languages) are subject to a greater fluidity (or sometimes with a disruption) of cultural identity, learning to switch between cultural contexts. This makes the identification of heart music more difficult. However, while today's globalized context is more complex, it also means, positively for intercultural worship, greater potential for sharing across heart musics.

Second, others assert that people acculturate, or become 'socialized', to a church community partly through its music (Marti, pp. 80–3). They learn to worship in this style. This is also true and has been so through the ages. Nonetheless, it overlooks the neuroscience almost completely and risks falling into a neo-colonialist, assimilationist approach that expects worshippers to fit in with 'our' musical culture, accentuating the cultural privileging of some and the marginalization of others.

A third objection is also valid, that focusing on heart music risks worship becoming individualized and consumer-centric. As we have seen, intercultural worship should promote the exact opposite: a communal sense of a new shared worship culture. We might think that emphasizing an individual or cultural group's musical preferences could detract from the congregation's corporate expression. While this could be true, by overlooking a particular expression we are choosing somebody else's heart expression instead. Rather, if a community hears and participates in an individual or group's heart expression, those people feel valued and the whole community is being shaped, gradually growing in its appreciation of God and these people.

In summary, heart music is complex because musical preferences arise from many factors. Psychologists recognize the primary importance of our childhood and adolescence but other factors are personality, age, values, context of music (function, activity, time of day), exposure to and education about music (Heshmat), gender (Colley) and genetics (Copenhagen). None of the above arguments against heart music diminish the intrinsic power of the right kinds of music on people's worshipping hearts. The question is: 'What music forms will we use in our setting to bring as many people as possible together?'

Worshipping with a Variety of Heart Music Styles

What, then, is practically possible in churches? The missionary ethnomusicologist Dr Roberta King spent many years in Africa and points to the damaging results of not paying attention to others' heart musics:

> *In practical terms, every ethnic group represented ... should, at some point ... have the opportunity to worship in ways that draw from their own heritage ... Without such inclusion, people are forced to deny certain aspects of themselves. (2005, p. 322)*

This is a sobering thought: our song choices may force people to 'deny certain aspects of themselves'. In speaking with others it is quite common for people to admit to missing certain ways of offering their prayer and praise. They feel they need to just accept what is offered and they need to fit into a church culture, even if it is not their own. This stark realization should cause us to ask: 'What culture is being privileged by the songs we sing?' In other words, if the heart music of each worshipper is not represented at some points in the life of the church, it can cause a feeling of 'foreignness', even in the most mature believers in the most welcoming of churches. On the other hand, if leaders make wise choices and aspects of each person's heart music are included at some point, everyone can find their voice in worship.

Understanding Heart Music Counters Unconscious Bias

Many who design services do not generally consider the cultural preferences of their members, so it may be troubling to realize that, without intending it, they privilege *someone's* heart music with every song choice. The question is: *whose* heart music? Such choices can reveal an unintended but unconscious bias towards a cultural group (and therefore not towards others), often based on personal values. Understanding heart music, then, is the best way to avoid unconscious bias.

When to Discuss Heart Music (Not Just Before the Service!)

When is the right time to address heart music? There are two obvious forums for this. First, in leaders' meetings strategic discussions about heart music can be held long before any individual service is designed. These then inform general discussions about music choices in the worship and the overall song repertoire. Second, in periodic music rehearsals (not final pre-meeting run-throughs), where musicians meet to share fellowship and learn new songs, where arrangements are tried out and the team can enjoy these songs for themselves well before they bring them to the congregation.

Balancing Different Heart-Music Songs

If there are fifty people in your church, or five hundred or five thousand, there are as many heart-music preferences. How do we handle this? Initially we can find overlaps that will work. This is relatively easy to identify because it probably includes your current repertoire. Then, how can we tailor-make other heart-music preferences?

There is a delicate balance:

- If we overemphasize shared heart-music styles, distinctive voices will be lost.
- If we overemphasize distinctive voices, it will marginalize others.

Joy Kim of the Proskuneo community has expressed this balance well:

> *In multicultural settings, Western musical styles that are already one part of people's heart musics may become a common factor shared by the participants. But musics and languages of their cultures are also unique contributing factors for each participant. (p. 134)*

In practice, this results in *two or three* categories of heart music to consider.

Shared Heart Music

From my own church experience, I agree with Kim that there is often a globalized style of worship music that many in the church are familiar with. It is possibly the church's default style, such as Christian contemporary music, gospel music, a liturgical tradition, a choral hymn style or some combination of genres. This forms an existing widely appreciated body of songs. We can extend the use of this common canon of songs by diversifying languages used. This can be a win–win, an easy first step.

Culturally Distinct Heart Music

There will almost always be songs that represent particular people and groups. It is easy to overlook this because we think it is too different. However, embracing these is a way to grow in worship. Usually they can be sung by the congregation with all participating. However, if any are too challenging, ways can be found to engage with this, such as the person or group presenting or playing a video of it at a suitable moment at a special event.

Newly Composed Heart Music

Additionally, for musically gifted groups, a third strand of repertoire is that of songs created together. Kim provides a fascinating example of this, where one participant in the collaboration:

> brought with him a traditional instrumental performer and a keyboard with Arabic quarter-tones because it showed that he felt free to include them, that the instruments would fit with the songs people created together, even though the songs also drew from other languages and cultural elements. He considered the song to be representative of both himself and the group. (p. 134)

The key observation in this example is that the player of Arabic music felt his musical contribution was included.

 ## A Heart-Music Survey

How can we best go about finding out what heart musics exist in our congregation? Below is a simple three-part survey that can be used in your church. From experience, it can be an enjoyable exercise, resulting in laughter, relationship-building, growing mutual appreciation and self-understanding. It does not have to become over-technical. Regard this as 'taking the temperature' of people's musical preferences rather than a university research project! On the other hand, I recommend that this should be prepared well. First, a pilot survey could be done by a smaller group (such as the musicians). After that you can iron out any ambiguities or confusions for your wider audience. The survey could be conducted by someone used to collecting data because it is important that the way the survey is introduced does not skew the answers in a particular direction.

Considerations When Conducting a Heart-Music Survey

1. This survey is an important aspect of listening well.
2. Church leaders and musicians need to be open to receive the results.
3. Emphasize to participants that their musical examples should not just be music they like but music that impacts them most deeply.
4. Guide people's minds away from thinking only about worship, asking: 'What is the music you are most moved by in life as a whole?'
5. Helpful questions to prompt answers include:
   - If you use playlists or voice activated devices, what music do you select?
   - What film or radio music touches you most?
   - What music do you find yourself suddenly responding to (positively)?
   - What music might represent 'you' at your anniversary, wedding or funeral?
6. Some people feel they don't understand music well. Assure them that there is no pressure for them to do this. For various reasons, some people do not 'think musically'.[2] Others may

---

[2] A small percentage cannot mentally recall a melody or someone's voice. They have a condition now identified as *anauralia*.

need a few examples. Generally there will be enough people in the church to get a helpful overview of heart-music preferences.
7. Ask participants to include examples (names, audio or video links) to help clarify their answers wherever possible.
8. Feel free to adapt the sample survey or design your own. Use paper or web-based survey technology. The survey could equally be held in a discussion-group format.
9. Manage expectations well. Clarify that the survey is part of a listening exercise and is *not* intended to result in everybody's top songs being automatically included. Leaders still have responsibility to shape worship for the benefit of all and the results will help them identify where the Lord may be leading.
10. The survey needs to observe data-protection protocols, including simple written permissions for appropriate data use.

Three-Part Survey

The survey comes in three parts. Ask people to fill this in as honestly as possible, thinking about the broadest range of music in their lives. For 'priority' columns, respondents can place a number '1' to show which of these examples is most important.

The second part is intended to cover the whole range of songs a person has ever used for their own private devotions or in a church service. They can be from any country, church, generation, language or culture that they have experienced.

Third, ask participants to think of their home language (spoken), personal prayer language (speaking or thinking) and the language they prefer for singing.

Your Heart Music

(Think about ALL the types of music you have in your life)

What music most ...	*Think of music that helps you when you are ...*	*Music example* (Audio or video link if possible)
1 *Relaxes you?* (your 'comfort' music)	Feeling stressed, sad or sick/falling asleep or waking up	
2 *Energizes you?* (your 'active' music)	Exercising or doing practical jobs	
3 *Feels like your musical best friend?* (your 'identity' music)	Expressing yourself on your own (e.g. in the shower/walking for pleasure)	

Your Three Top Christian Songs of all Time

(From any country, in any language and musical style)

1
2
3

Language Preferences

What language(s) do you prefer to use at home, in private prayer and singing songs?

87

AN INTERCULTURAL WORSHIP HANDBOOK

 **Analysing the Survey**

One of the aims of this book is to help us avoid unintended assumptions about what other people find helpful in worship. Therefore this survey is designed to reveal options. To help make sense of the results you can draw up a list showing people's priorities.

Questions after the Survey

1. Does it look as if questions were clearly understood?
2. What percentage affirmed the church's current worship music?
3. What percentage listed other worship-music styles?
4. How many people listed specific genres of music?
5. What percentage might prefer current songs but with other languages?
6. What specific songs were listed?
7. What languages were listed?

Implications of the Survey Results

1. What are your biggest surprises? What do these tell you?
2. What do the results say to affirm your current music style?
3. What additional musical styles would be appreciated?
4. What 'top Christian song' ideas could be incorporated?
5. What language adjustments are suggested by this?
6. What other adjustments to corporate worship practice could be implied?
7. Was anything listed that could be used for events outside regular worship?

Follow-Up Discussions

After the survey it would be good to hold another discussion to consider what the survey indicates by way of direction and next steps. The survey is intended to gather information, to help include musical worship that reflects all participants. How we go about implementing changes is as important as making them. Ephesians 4.15–16, quoted elsewhere, shows us the way intercultural worship grows. Specifically, we will grow into a united and mature body of Christ as we love one another, accept one another as equals and give space for 'each part' to 'do its work'. As a result, our worship will gradually begin to look, sound and feel more diverse, fuller, more enriching and more honouring of Christ who is the head of the church.

 Questions to Ponder

1 How could understanding your own heart music help in your personal worship life?
2 What benefits could this understanding have on your corporate worship?
3 Would it help your worship community to conduct a simple heart-music survey? If so, how and when?

7

Appreciating: Cultural Ways of Encountering God

In the last two chapters I have addressed questions of musical diversity and heart music, but culturally diverse worship is not simply about songs that are sung. It also about the total context of those songs that make them special to those whose heart music they represent. In our Oldham church the majority culture missed this. We learned the songs of the cultures who joined us but did not understand how they were done in their original settings. The way we did them was rather tame and anglicized! Thankfully, liberal doses of love and support were being shared and, as Peter says, 'love covers over a multitude of sins' (1 Pet. 4.8). This shows that trying something and reaching out across cultures goes a long way – because intercultural worship is first about genuine relationships. This chapter, then, is about understanding the worship backgrounds believers come from.

Cultural Ways of Worshipping God

Whether we are conscious of it or not, all worship meetings come with a set of cultural values. Our experience of church reflects this, from the greetings, refreshments and offering, to sermon illustrations, how we address leaders and our approach to time. We come with mental maps of how things should be done. Most of this is shaped by church tradition. Some of it is theological but a large part is shaped by culture – and because culture is like the air we breathe, we are least conscious of it. Often it is only when we experience another culture's worship that we start noticing differences. This is one of the most liberating features of intercultural worship but we may also discover resistance in our hearts. This can be a little alarming as we grow aware how entrenched we have become, which is why we spent time earlier discussing listening. Intercultural church is very healthy for discipleship! It involves facing our feelings as we interact across cultures. This will help us move forward. It will free us to worship together in ways that honour God and one another. As 1 Peter 2.17 says: 'Show proper respect to everyone, love the family of believers, fear God.'

How, then, can we distinguish between various cultural ways of worshipping God? One tool is the 'Grid of Cultural Preferences in a Worship Meeting' (Figure 3). I have adapted this from the 'Cultural Values Continuum' chart by Sandra Maria Van Opstal, to whom I am indebted (Van Opstal, pp. 179–181). In this grid the focus is on how culture impacts a worship meeting. Ways to make use of this resource are also given below. The suggestions put forward are intended for leaders to hold deeper conversations with a group of church members from a variety of cultures. This exercise is not usually something for the whole church but for key voices who can communicate honestly and clearly. When using this grid, think especially about a typical meeting for a church's regular congregational worship. The grid highlights common differences to help you consider what cultural emphases help various members of your church. The outcome of this is likely to help you identify attitudes and practices that will help the worship of the church to be more suitable for more people.

How to Use the Grid

Gather a group of people who will be able to represent enough different cultural voices.

AN INTERCULTURAL WORSHIP HANDBOOK

Grid of Cultural Preferences in a Worship Meeting

100%	50%	0%
FORMAL	Describe the general atmosphere (example: Am I free to laugh or interrupt?)	INFORMAL
PLANNED	How much of the meeting is planned? How much is spontaneous?	UNPLANNED
TEACHING	How much do speakers give principles or use stories and illustrations?	STORY
FRONT-LED	How much is led by service leaders? How much do others contribute?	GROUP INPUT
REVERENT	How much is expression emotionally reverent and reflective? How much is passionate?	PASSIONATE
TALKING	How much time is spent on talking? How much on singing?	SINGING
STILLNESS	How much bodily expression is still? How much uses movement?	MOVEMENT
I–YOU language	How much do notices, talks, songs, prayer etc. use 'I' language? How much uses 'We'?	WE–US language
PLAIN communication	Does communication mainly use plain language or the arts, metaphors and symbols?	SYMBOLIC* communication
DIRECT	How direct are speakers in calling for response?	INDIRECT
CLOCK TIME	How much do meetings start/end on set times? How much when people are ready?	EVENT TIME
EGALITARIAN	In public speech, are personal first names used or are titles and family names used?	HIERARCHICAL

*'Symbolic' – how much symbolism is used? The Bible, songs, sermons and the arts are full of symbolism (such as word pictures like 'refuge' or 'washing'). Understanding it requires familiarity with cultural or theological meanings.

© 2020 Ian Collinge. Inspired by Sandra Maria Van Opstal, *The Next Worship: Glorifying God in a Diverse World* (IVP Books, 2016, pp. 178–81).

Figure 3

Example: Formal – Informal

Let's take the top line. You can fill out the grid using the same method for each line. People can compare what they are accustomed to from their backgrounds or plot their current church. Both would be instructive. Some types of church like to be quite formal while others value informality. One way to identify levels of formality might be to consider how free congregation members are to 'interrupt' speakers with a question or comment, or to laugh. Dress code or liturgical text style may demonstrate formality or informality. This is a subjective exercise but it can show important variations.

 Drawing Your Profiles

For each church and for each characteristic:

- Mark with a dot where your worship culture fits on each spectrum.
- Join the dots with lines to reveal a profile shape (as below).

The comparison below shows a church I knew in Europe (Figure 4) and another in Asia (Figure 5). The former is on the left side; the latter is more communal, more indirect in challenging, more event-orientated and more hierarchical in relationships. We can see these distinctions immediately.

AN INTERCULTURAL WORSHIP HANDBOOK

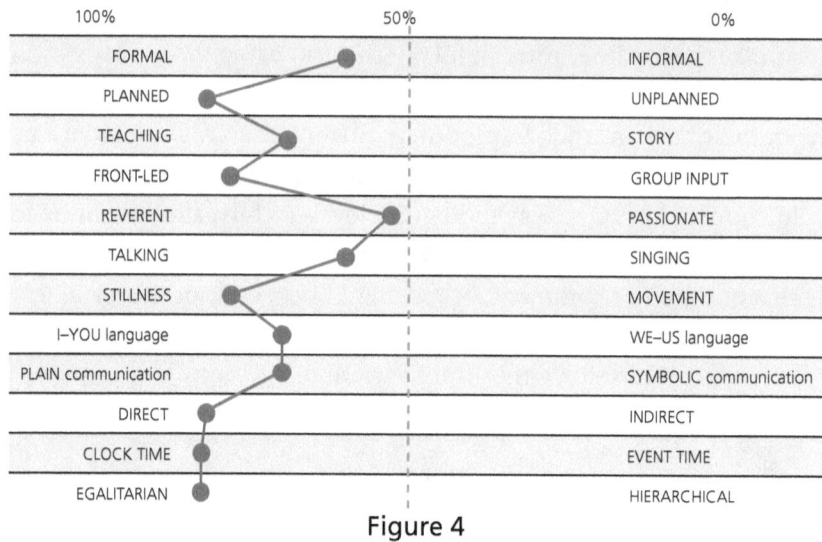

Figure 4

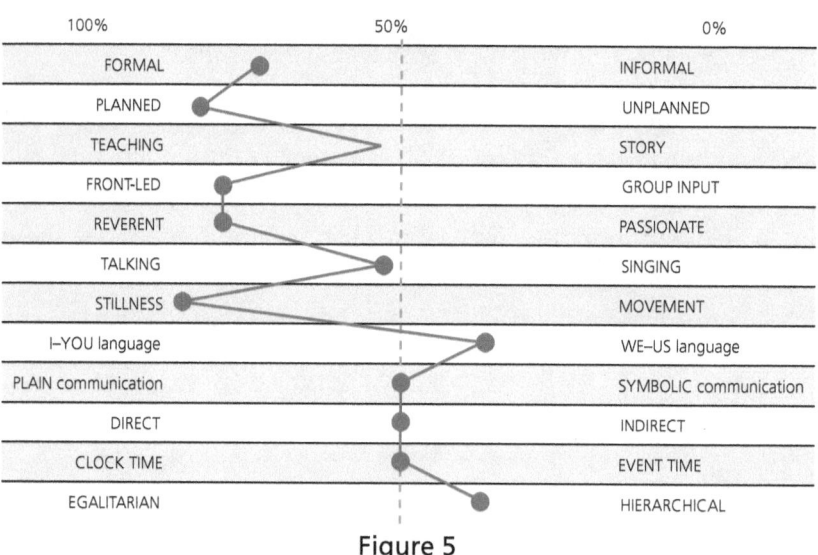

Figure 5

If you do this as a group discussion, make this a listening exercise. You could watch video material to help illustrate profiles. Please note: this is not a competition! It is not a case of one culture being more godly, biblical or spiritual. Rather, share reasons and values behind the answers to grow your intercultural understanding. Look for the gold in each, asking: 'Where is the image of God expressed especially clearly?' Eventually, you can use your insights to develop intercultural worship in your church. For example, expressive cultures may learn the value of stillness, while formal cultures may learn to appreciate a greater level of informality.

A Few Aspects of Culture in Worship

Next, we focus on a few ways that cultural preferences are expressed, inspired by Sandra Maria Van Opstal's concept of 'worship cultures' (pp. 62–75; 201–6; 121–2). These show the kinds of questions that could inform your conversations. They are only a sample and represent just four cultural church groupings common in Britain: Black Majority Churches, East Asian (Chinese and South Korean), Persian and White Majority. For your context, you can expand this to cultures you have contact with. These observations add some details to what we learned from the grid, drawn mainly from what cultural insiders and expert outsiders have expressed, mostly in personal communications with me. Here we hear their voices – individuals more familiar than I am with these cultures.

Cautions about Cultural Preferences

1 Please do not stereotype anyone into cultural boxes!
2 Please ask people about their specific preferences and experiences. A good question is: 'In your culture (or 'From your perspective'), what does worship look, sound and feel like?'
3 Each culture is far fuller, deeper and more complex than any one description. Please do not regard the comments below as complete or universally relevant. People from the same culture and different generations are likely to give different answers.
4 Develop questions for your own contexts. The observations below are here to inspire ideas for discussion.

Some Cultural Approaches

Despite these warnings, there is great value in what the people quoted below have contributed and I thank each of them for sharing with me.

Planning and Flexibility

As we saw on the worship and culture grid above, planning is important for some cultures, particularly western culture, possibly reflecting the 'Protestant work ethic'. For others, flexibility is vital. As Van Opstal says of White Majority churches:

> *Songs are often done in a similar way every time. There may be some repetition, but it is usually planned out by the band ahead of time, and the general order of the song rarely changes. (p. 206)*

With such a fundamental difference, each multi-ethnic church needs to find a sweet spot that works for their people. Rather than 'timekeepers' frowning on the 'flexible' or the latter considering detailed planners 'unspiritual', open-minded conversations help everyone find the right balance.

Use of the Bible in Expressive Worship

There are many ways to convey biblical truth. The following three are used in all cultures but emphases vary and intercultural worship can incorporate the benefits of each.

1 Truth Through Song

Many recognize that worshippers learn theology in song. Western-style hymns and songs can be lyrically rich but text-dense, appealing to the educated and literate. This can inadvertently exclude people who struggle with this level of language. In intercultural worship, we can convey truth using a variety of styles, languages, formats and levels of complexity.

2 Truth Though Storytelling

Storytelling is a great way to engage congregations. Rob Baker, a lecturer in African ethnomusicology, says of worship in West Africa that the 'leader (caller) … *communicates* with the congregation with great energy, as though telling them a story, or exhorting them to join in'. Jonah Ulebor, a British Nigerian, illustrates this:

> *common biblical themes that inspire praise and worship that you will often hear from praise leaders: Paul and Silas in the prison, David's Dance, God's Charge to Jehoshaphat not to fight but lead with the Levites and singers.*

Intercultural worship and service leaders could incorporate short stories – whether spontaneous or pre-prepared.

3 Truth Through Poetry

Biblical psalms and Christian songs use poetic structures and imagery. This is noticeable in the Chinese Canaan Hymns. Several Iranian believers[1] have indicated to me that Persians value poetry in everyday conversation and worship. In Oldham we shared a beautiful poem about Christ by Gherajeh Da'aghi, read in Farsi, projecting the Persian script and English interpretation on a screen:

> *O How Fortunate those who recognize and accept the Liberating Love of the Prince of Peace, Saviour of the World, Jesus Christ.*

---

1 Names withheld for their security.

Texts like this are not only worshipful but evangelistic. For both reasons, then, biblical truth is perhaps more captivating for Persians if read or sung as poetry. Let's remember, Jesus and the apostles made use of poetry (Matt. 11.17; Acts 17.28).

Reverence and Passion

In any culture, some like to be reflective and others like outward expression. Intercultural churches can make space for this diversity – in appropriate ways. Let's look at two: exuberant passion and quiet reverence.

Worship in Black Majority Churches is often described as 'passionate'. Dr Daniel Akhazemea paints this picture:

> *The worship experience in a black majority church is characterized by exuberant worship, clapping and dancing, the preaching is quite dynamic and centred on meeting the social, religious and cultural needs of their members.* (p. 24)

On the other hand, for some East Asians the preference may be towards 'reverence'. Jessie Tang reports a 'quiet intensity' in her London Chinese church. The UK-based Singaporean musician Hilary Kemp agrees:

> *Asian worship does ... have an emphasis on quieter moments and creating space for personal intimacy with God, which is something I ... try to recreate in church with my [keyboard] playing.*

Tears

The Korean American ethnodoxologists Jaewoo and Joy Kim highlight that, for some Koreans, 'Good worship is often measured by emotional intensity which may result in tears.' Older Koreans say they have received 'grace' (*Eun-Hye*) when their worship is experienced at this depth. Likewise, some Persians describe worship as an emotional, inner experience of deep closeness with the God who has loved you in Christ, who suffered on the cross for your sins, has forgiven you and has set you free. This too can result in tears of gratitude, joy and a release from burdens such as anxiety, trauma and unforgiveness. God takes note of our tears, whether of sadness or joy (2 Kings 20.5; Job 16.20; Ps. 56.8, 126.5; Isa. 38.5; Jer. 9.1; Lam. 2.11; John 11.33; Acts 20.19), so intercultural churches can create an atmosphere where each can worship in their own way.

Dance and Movement

In contrast with their religious background, some Persians discover that they are allowed to be joyful in God's presence, including communal dancing, if their church permits it. Some African denominations may prohibit dance but dance is important to others. Jonah Ulebor remarks that, in Nigeria, dance is:

> *a very important aspect of worship and you are not known to be grateful if your body is not moving, I think that comes from a cultural viewpoint that gratitude should be obvious especially to a big God.*

Physical movement in worship is not restricted to certain cultures. In South Korea, I observed a student body who intentionally broke out of cultural restraints with loud worship music, moving energetically around the room, one blowing a football whistle. This illustrates that scope for sharing across cultural preferences is not as limited as it may appear and freedom in a mix of responses can be encouraged.

Individual or Communal Response

Jessie Tang agrees with Van Opstal (Opstal, p. 203) that the role of Asian worship leaders is 'invitation':

> *for my church, the Chinese service will always sit and stand at the same time. They need to be invited to do so ... It has to be a collective thing. (Tang, 2020)*

Non-Asian church leaders, then, need to consider that while some Asians are happy in individualistic settings, others prefer a communal invitation.

Musical Elements

With resources on the internet there is no lack of materials for intercultural worship. What musical elements might be important for your range of cultures? Coco Mbassi, an award-winning French-Cameroonian singer songwriter, describes music in African worship:

> *I would characterize some of the urban worship in Africa as westernized with an African twist, in the genre, accompaniment, or ... rhythms that characterize African musical styles. This is because in larger population centres, musicians are formally trained, often to a very high standard, and conversant in various musical styles from jazz, gospel, to pop or rock et cetera, they can do anything really. ... Instruments include guitar, bass, keys, drumset, percussions, and vocals (backing and lead) are very prominent and important. Elements of call of response can be present, as well as lead singers improvising over the melody and main lyrics ... sung by backing vocalists, a choir where relevant, and the congregation.*

Jonah Ulebor highlights harmonies in Nigerian urban worship:

> *Singing in 'different parts' and creating harmony ... is considered an important part in African worship. Most choirs spend significant time in 'blending' and making sure sopranos, alto and tenors sing in a way that is musically complementary (harmony).*

APPRECIATING

By contrast, Jessie Tang describes Chinese congregational worship as 'very piano-led, with multiple singers singing the tune, not many harmonies at all (if any)':

> *There's always a lack of instrumentalists but enough singers, ... Most songs have the same style – piano-led, introduction, singing in the same structure that is normal for the song, with a repeated last line slowing down to end. (2020)*

Chinese-language services include translated hymns and contemporary English-language music, along with Chinese brands, such as *Stream of Praise, River of Life Christian Church* and *Melody of My Heart*. The Cantonese congregation can, of course, access Cantonese material:

> *Their multifaceted approach flows into their musical style: energetic, with a combination of gospel, Mandopop and Cantopop'. (Tang, 2018, p. 5)*

For Persians, there are Farsi-language songs and translations from Arabic, Armenian, Assyrian and English. The website Kalameh of Elim Ministries provides a song archive. Persian worship is almost always in what westerners call 'minor' keys, undoubtedly influenced by Persian traditional musical aesthetics.

About White Majority Worship in the USA, Van Opstal says:

> *White/Western worship encompasses many different genres of music including modern rock, hymns and folk ... The volume usually depends on the generations represented; people do, however, like to hear themselves sing. (p. 206)*

In British worship in the 2020s, hearing oneself sing seems to be less expected. In contemporary churches the music team includes guitar, keyboard, bass guitar and drums, with a lead singer and support singer(s). Some add orchestral instruments such as violin, cello, saxophone or flute. Most contemporary songs are in major keys using a small range of chords and in four time, with a handful in six time (6/8). Older hymns like the three-time 'Be Thou My Vision' are often given a contemporary arrangement in four time.

Intercultural churches, then, can embrace a variety of musical styles as music teams expand their skills and new people are incorporated. This happens step by step. Inviting a Nigerian drummer to play highlife rhythm, a Persian to lead a Farsi song or a gospel choir to 'raise a hallelujah' in harmony helps everyone feel a connection as we hear people's hearts in worship.

Is it Really Possible to Combine Cultural Preferences?

Combining diversity with unity may not be as stark a choice as we may first imagine. Let us consider the following.

Intercultural Expressions Are Not Unusual

Many believers are willing to embrace greater diversity. First, in a culturally diverse country, many are already familiar with cross-cultural encounters and expressions. Second, it is natural for humans to enjoy variety. As Ecclesiastes 3 says, 'There is a time for everything, and a season for every activity under the heavens':

> a time to weep and a time to laugh, a time to mourn and a time to dance ... a time to embrace and a time to refrain from embracing ... a time to be silent and a time to speak. (vv. 1, 4, 5b, 7b)

Intercultural Synergy

As we experiment with diverse worship, imaginative and creative collaborations become the incubator for a worship environment that fits our congregation. Here we are not only looking for *addition* – Culture A + Culture B + Culture C. Rather, we are looking for *synergy*

– a new mix, made up of the various components but in a way that has possibly never existed before. This is where we need the Holy Spirit to create something fresh. The key lies in recognizing that, if we want God to bring this about, we need to hold less tightly to some of our old patterns and be willing to draw in others to add their textures to the mix, allowing the body to grow 'as each part does its work' (Eph. 4.16).

 **Next Steps**

If this synergy is to happen, what steps can you take? For example, why not discuss the range of cultural preferences represented in your church? You could devote a relaxed day or a couple of evenings to this, to consult selected representatives of various cultures – preferably with multi-ethnic food! Have each person illustrate their most important values by playing audio or video examples.

Some important questions might be those below.

Worship Questions for a Church Cultural Diversity Group

1 What does the worship of Jesus in your culture look, sound and feel like?
2 How can our church help you express your worship?
3 What are the most important features to introduce first?
4 What changes, if any, might need to be made to our current practice?

Of course, any changes need to be introduced well and gradually, with respect given to all groups in the church. The process also needs to maintain momentum, not stagnate. May the Lord give you wisdom not only for the vision but also for the process!

Questions to Ponder

1 What tools or steps might be helpful to enable your church or organization to embrace a wider palette of cultural expressions?
2 What cultural expressions of worship are represented by people in your setting? How can you discover these?

8

Creating: Putting Flesh on the Bones

Speaking the Vision into Being

> *Then he said to me, 'Prophesy to these bones and say to them, "Dry bones, hear the word of the LORD! This is what the Sovereign LORD says to these bones: I will make breath enter you, and you will come to life. I will attach tendons to you and make flesh come upon you and cover you with skin; I will put breath in you, and you will come to life. Then you will know that I am the LORD."' (Ezek. 37.4-6)*

Our 'Flesh on the Bones' Moment

In Ezekiel's vision there came the moment when God put flesh on the bones. In this picture we see God at work – and it is exhilarating. Such a point can come in our churches too! When we begin to express our cultural diversity with real people, real languages, real songs and real engagement with God and fellow worshippers, that's a watershed. It's a 'flesh on the bones' moment, a sign of the kingdom of God at work among us. The other amazing factor is that God loves to involve us in the process of his miracle-working. Ezekiel is told to 'prophesy', to speak the word of the Lord to the bones. This is Ezekiel's role. Our role too is to speak intercultural worship into being.

You don't have to understand everything before you take the first or next step. In fact it's best simply to come to God in prayer and then start walking in obedience to the vision. In our Oldham church we didn't know what we needed to do. We merely prayed for God to change the colour of our church and God brought Osman. A few weeks later, our 'flesh on the bones' moment came when Osman taught us a song from Sierra Leone and the congregation joined in with his worship. It was a thrilling experience. It gave confidence that we could worship with this song – and with more like it! This was not a complicated process. In one way it was incredibly easy – but it began a journey of experimenting, creating, adapting and improving over several years. Then more people came from other cultures. All this resulted in our worship moving from monocultural to multicultural and eventually moving towards intercultural. Changes in sung worship were symbolic of a bigger change: they expressed the growing openness of church members to embrace people of many cultures.

'Speaking to the bones' will mean three things:

1 *Hearing* from God about the vision.
2 *Speaking* about it to those involved.
3 *Taking action* (such as a song, prayer or reading in someone's mother tongue from a culture other than the church's majority).

Everything else can follow, including most of the tools advocated in this book. These should help you to keep on track and also help if you're feeling stuck. I advocate a learning-on-the-go approach, a prayerful, praise-filled pilgrimage with fellow travellers, taking time to savour each experience together.

Getting Practical

This chapter is about the process of designing worship to reflect who we are in our varied personal, cultural and church identities. Previously we learned four key activities from musicians collaborating in cross-cultural musical creativity. Now we will apply these to our own contexts:

CREATING

Four Cross-Cultural Creative Activities

1 Listening (to other voices).
2 Connecting (hearts, minds and ideas).
3 Creating (together).
4 Celebrating (cultural diversity).

 ## Listening and Connecting

It is good for music leaders and service planners to come together – ideally in culturally diverse groups – to listen to and connect with each other about songs and other elements that can be used in communal worship. This listening is an intentional intercultural activity, seeking to hear and not just to be heard. From this should flow connecting – as humans and fellow worshippers, sharing heart to heart in story, song, ideas and other means. Most of the tools in this book are designed to help the listening process. Where there are not yet sufficient people of other cultures to listen to and connect with, why not discuss what languages and ethnic groups represent your priorities – whether those attending church or communities you have a vision to reach? At this point the question about resources will most naturally relate to materials that are already available, such as those mentioned later in this chapter.

 ## Creating

As we take steps together, we can listen, connect and research materials.

AN INTERCULTURAL WORSHIP HANDBOOK

> **Discovering and Working on Materials**
>
> 1 Songs can emerge to learn and prepare for church worship.
> 2 Songs can be translated and arranged, where needed.
> 3 We can learn why these songs are important to people.
> 4 We can discover something about the way these songs are done in the person's former churches.
> 5 We can discover what other worship practices are meaningful to others.
> 6 We can discover people able to collaborate to create songs and other resources.

 **Celebrating**

Let's enjoy learning from one another and being enriched by each of these song traditions. Laying aside pride in our own cultures and our assumptions about what we think makes a song or a practice good, we will be able to value each worship tradition on its own terms, to embrace the different, not as inferior but as another gift from God. Let's celebrate every sign of God's hand in each cultural expression.

Creative Spaces

Let's find those resources, take steps to try things out and make time to do so! As we saw above, and now see, the next verse of Ezekiel shows how God acts as we do our bit:

> *So I prophesied as I was commanded. And as I was prophesying, there was a noise, a rattling sound, and the bones came together, bone to bone. I looked, and tendons and flesh appeared on them and skin covered them, but there was no breath in them. (Ezek. 37.7–8)*

'Rattling' is such an evocative word. It's the sound of activity, humans responding to the breath of God. Ezekiel is the one who speaks but the tendons and flesh are newly created by God. If our efforts are to unite the tribes, if the church is going to arise with fresh energy and if this will give God the glory that alone can come from his diverse people, we need the breath of God. This points to a prayerful openness to God – as we listen, connect, create, experiment and joyfully celebrate our cultural diversity. Below are a few ways to generate musical and other materials. The formats mentioned here work well together; they are not mutually exclusive. Consider which ones will work best in your setting.

1 Workshops

A workshop is a good first step and best run by a specialist or small team. The facilitator could be a consultant from outside or a gifted facilitator from within the church. Ideally this person is not usually the one to create new material, rather is good at drawing others out. They may also know where to find resources and may spot talent others have not seen.

Components of Intercultural Worship Workshops

- *Interactive Teaching* about reasons for intercultural worship.
- *Honest Discussion* about gaps in current repertoire and resources (songs and other items).
- *Mutual Sharing* of songs participants know and other ideas for inclusion in services.
- *Creative Experimentation*: working on new songs, possible arrangements and other materials.
- *Sketching Plans*: how these items could be integrated into services.

2 Creative Jam Sessions

Jam sessions are free-flowing opportunities to share songs and create together. They can be held on a regular basis every few weeks or months. They can be separate or included as a part of regular music practices. They can include song learning but with the freedom to be creative. If those responsible generate an atmosphere that gives everyone the freedom to experiment, the potential can be wonderfully life-giving. This format need not be limited to musicians. It can also work for other collaborative artistic creativity, such as visual art, dance moves, spoken-word creation and so on. The beautiful reality is that even though the focus is on human creativity, you may experience moments when you realize that it's not just *your* creativity but that, as Jesus says, *he* loves to be present as well when we gather in his name.

3 Regular Meetings for Creative Exploration

After any of these activities, it is easy for creative activity to come to a stop. One way to guard against this is to agree to meet once every three or four months to engage in creativity – with a format and frequency that people can sustain. This is a way to ensure that new materials can be discovered, developed or created and it's a context for newer arrivals to add their own voices and gifts.

An Affirming Atmosphere for Creativity

Above all, the most important ingredient is to generate a community of mutual encouragement. It is surprising what can happen in such an atmosphere. Whether you have many or few creatives, it is good to provide a way to release each person to use their gifts in church life. Unfortunately this is not always the case. Intentionality is important. The key aspect is trust. If people feel that they will be affirmed and not constantly 'corrected', they are more likely to have a go; they do not have to be a professional. This group might also spark creativity by individuals, pairs or groups. Let's rejoice in all such desire to create for God! In the mid-1980s, a church I pastored in Central London included musicians with experience of writing songs. We celebrated these songs and sang them along with songs of the time. Gradually a warm atmosphere of creative encouragement developed and more people wrote songs, including some who would never consider themselves songwriters. Sometimes a song was developed as a group. What emerged over time was an expression of worship that represented the unique voices of the church – a new shared worship culture. This example points to the importance of three postures needed to spark creativity, whether in a workshop, a jamming session or service planning meetings.

Three Postures for Healthy Creativity

1 Build a positive, safe atmosphere, with freedom to fail as well as succeed.
2 Rely on the Holy Spirit.
3 Be persistent and patient.

As with Ezekiel, the energizing process did not happen all at once. He needed to prophesy more than once and we too need to be God-reliant, proactive, persistent and patient. The encouragement to press on with creativity usually needs to be repeated. Once again, Ezekiel was instructed to speak, to see things come to life:

Then he said to me, 'Prophesy to the breath; prophesy, son of man, and say to it, "This is what the Sovereign LORD *says: Come, breath, from the four winds and breathe into these slain, that they may live."' So I prophesied as he commanded me, and breath entered them; they came to life and stood up on their feet. (Ezek. 37.9–10)*

Paul describes New Testament prophecy in this way: 'the one who prophesies speaks to people for their strengthening, encouraging and comfort' (1 Corinthians 14.3). We too can speak into one another's lives for spiritual and mutual support.

 ## Building Your Resources

The purpose of these activities is to learn, arrange or generate new intercultural resources. Let's now look at discovering and arranging suitable songs.

1 Finding Songs

Learn a song from a church member

This is exactly how our Oldham church started on intercultural worship. The pastor invited our very first asylum seeker to teach us a song from his background. Fortunately, he was sensitive to choose an English-language song and one that fitted well with our church. This was followed by similar songs in English. After this he agreed to teach us one in Krio. When East Africans and Iranians arrived, we learned songs from them too. It's worth noting that sometimes we needed either to learn something new (such as the leader and echo format), reduce the number of verses or add an English translation.

Add languages to familiar songs

Another easy first step is to take songs you know already and add a short refrain in another language (a chorus, bridge or other section) – a language relevant to your church and not difficult to pronounce. Initially, learn this from a native-language speaker. The leader can invite people to take a moment to reflect and to listen as 'our friend sings this in her own language'. If this person is not confident to sing it in public, a linguistically minded singer can take that role, making sure to learn the correct pronunciation. Later you can select a

CREATING

song with a slightly longer section in another language – such as a three- or four-line verse. The reason for this slowly-slowly approach is that, from my experience, it is best to avoid placing a heavy language demand on a congregation in English-speaking majority churches. Mother-tongue English speakers sometimes need time to gain confidence to sing in other languages. Singing it together means we can hide in the crowd while having a go. If songs are repeated sufficiently often, worshippers will feel more comfortable with the song and the words may stick in their heads.

Finding translations of English songs

The following are some examples.

Some Ways to Find Song Translations

1. The Songs2Serve website provides links to translations of well-known worship songs.
2. 'Waymaker' by Sinach (Osinachi Kalu Okoru Egbu) has been sung in at least 50 languages (K-Love).
3. 'How Great is Our God' by Chris Tomlin, Jesse Reeves and Ed Cash, exists in many languages (Passion Music).
4. For traditional hymns, there are many well-known and accepted translations (Ethnic Harvest; Hymnary.org).

Use short, repetitive songs from other cultures

Alongside familiar songs it is good to learn short songs from other cultures, especially repetitive songs. They can be used as prayer refrains, acclamations and songs of praise. A Krio language 'Thank you, Father' song that Osman introduced to the Oldham church is 'Tel am tenki, tel am' ('Tell him thank you'). It is extremely well known in Sierra Leone (One World; Cee-Jay). The fact that English speakers can hear hints of English is an advantage, and other West Africans may easily understand it. So there is little need of translation. There are only eleven words to this song, many of which repeat, making it accessible for most congregations.

Sing short refrains in original languages

Refrains (choruses or bridge sections) in other languages can work well for multi-ethnic congregations. A speaker of the original language might sing the longer sections (often the verses). The Hindi song 'Mukti Dilaye Yeshu Naam' can be done in this way. The chorus is sung in call-and-response form with everyone copying the leader. The verses can then be done by one or two people in Hindi. There are many arrangements of this song on the internet (Masihian; Phillips), but for an English-speaking congregation, one way is for the congregation to sing only the chorus and Hindi-speaking song leaders to sing the verses. Alternatively, musicians can play the verse.

> *Multi dilaye Yeshu naam. Shanti dilaye Yeshu naam (Hindi).*
> *Peace comes to you in Jesus' Name. Salvation in no other name (English echo).*

If you are searching for songs in other languages in contemporary styles, search the YouTube channels of Eric Lige and Proskuneo Ministries and the SongSelect (CCLI) website for songs in different languages.

'Songs in Hindi' by Sheldon Bangera appear on the SongSelect site. One is 'Ek Naam'. This is excellent for a dual-language version since it has separate Hindi and English versions (Jaago; Selah). This shows how worship musicians can be creative with arrangements even if a two-language arrangement is not available online. For example, the Resonance Band mix the two for a multi-ethnic setting. A solo lead singer sings the verses in English and the entire congregation sings a repeated refrain in Hindi: 'Yeshu hi Wo naam hai' ('Jesus is that name').

Learn multilingual songs

Some songs are already multilingual. These can be a great asset to a church learning how to be intercultural. Some of these have been translated into other languages while others started out as multilingual songs. I will mention four here.

'Hallelujah He's Alive'
This Sudanese song is featured by Proskuneo Ministries in a variety of languages, including ASL deaf signing. Different people can take the lead in each verse.

'I just want to say, Baba O Ese' ('Thank you, Father')
This well-known household favourite in Nigeria is bilingual in Yoruba and English. It can easily be adapted to other languages. (Arts Release, 2018)

'Multilingual Grace' by Proskuneo Ministries
Originally conceived as a song for giving thanks before a meal, this has become one of the most successful multilingual songs and is readily picked up by congregations. Verses are already available in English, Dutch, Korean, Arabic, Spanish, Burmese, Nepali, Swahili, Polish, Hebrew and Chinese. Its genius lies in a very simple chorus, with 'Thank you' in four languages followed by verses with matching 'thank you' words.

'Tribes' by Victory Worship in the Philippines
This powerful song for a rock-style worship band can be sung entirely in English or the national language Tagalog (Filipino), but the bridge can equally be sung in English with phrases in Tagalog and Spanish.

All these are examples of ways to mix languages.

AN INTERCULTURAL WORSHIP HANDBOOK

2 Song Languages

The first question for any song is how to use language, especially if the lyrics are long or difficult to pronounce. If so, you will need to adjust something to make them singable for your multicultural community. Typical questions are given below.

> ### Questions to Ask about Language Use in Songs
> - Which sections should the *whole congregation* sing?
> - Which sections should the *worship team* sing?
> - Which sections should *native speakers* of the language sing on their own?

Song sections

If the words are more demanding, a short, repeated refrain section can be taught to the congregation. The rest of the song can be sung by the leading group or choir. For example, the Resonance Band discovered that the verses of the Polish song 'Przyjaciela Mam' (Chrześcijańska) are challenging for English speakers but the chorus is much easier. In this instance, we can invite Polish speakers to sing the verse and then everyone can join the chorus. We also have an English setting of the verse for everyone to sing, so another way to do this is for the verse to be sung in English and the chorus in Polish.

Length of songs

Another adaptation has to do with the length of a song. It is typical in many African countries for songs to be repeated many times. The song 'Yesu Ni Wangu' is very well known in East Africa, and the version I was introduced to had seven verses in Swahili and seven equivalent verses in Luganda. If we add an English version to this, that will total twenty-one verses – rather long for British churches!

CREATING

For our setting, we reduced the number of verses. We now find most situations require one or two verses but in a mix of languages, such as Swahili, English and French or another language that church people speak (Arts Release, 2018).

Translating songs

If there is no existing translation for a proposed song, should you go ahead and make your own translation?

Questions About Translation

1. Contact the songwriter or copyright owners, wherever possible.
2. Check whether an official English version already exists somewhere.
3. For less complex lyrics, translate the song.
4. Find someone with a love of music and poetry to set the words.
5. Make the translation faithful and natural in the target language.

Should we translate songs at all?

Some say we should not translate songs at all. To some extent they are right – at a purely artistic level. When I listen to songs in other languages I enjoy the sound of the language as much as the music. The beauty of the song is interconnected with the beauty of the language. This is the paradox of the translator. The critics are right that translations can sometimes feel artificial and clunky, detracting from the beauty of the original. At the same time, we all know that translation is necessary for comprehension. The apostle Paul is clear about the need for interpretation in Christian worship (1 Cor. 14.13–19). This is our baseline for intercultural worship practice as well: our worship is multilingual but it must be understandable. If we want a concert or an aesthetic experience, we can leave songs untranslated. If we want to worship God with heart *and* mind, we need a translation.

Realistically, there are certain songs that just do not work in translation. These can be offered as a special contribution in the original language. Such translations usually don't work because the style is very different; they may be soloistic, with subtle vocal ornamentation that makes English translation awkward and group involvement difficult. Even in these cases, there is often a refrain that everyone can sing in one or both languages. If the song is too difficult for people to join in with, my advice would be to consider choosing a different song for congregational singing. Christian worship is essentially participatory. For this reason, despite imperfect translations this is no argument for leaving suitable songs untranslated. It is a reason to review and improve the translation.

Stylistic Features

Using 'Yesu Ni Wangu', mentioned above, as an example, this song clearly has a musical style that is accessible for western-style church musicians but is a little different from common English songs.

Call and Response and African Rhythms

- The song uses a call-and-response *pattern* common to several cultures. It is not complicated but it can confuse traditional English churchgoers if they think they need to sing everything all the time! They need to learn to listen to the leader and then repeat it: the lead singer sings a line solo, which the congregation then echoes. For this format, the choir or backing singers play a crucial role. They lead the congregation in when and what to sing.

CREATING

- One further difference with this song is that the *lead* singer sings the verse lines at a higher pitch from the response. For this, we clearly need a vocalist, group or choir to lead this *echo* part.

- The song also includes rhythmic and stylistic features that local church musicians will no doubt *adapt* to their own style and ability. The good thing is that it is equally possible for different musical groupings to lead this song, such as an unaccompanied choir with hand drums, or a band with guitar, keyboard, drums and voice.

- To add a more African vibe, interested musicians would do well to *add* to their skills. They could search out how different African groups cover this song, perhaps delving into certain rhythms, registers or timbres, such as the use of higher octaves, brighter organ stops or learning the Highlife rhythm and guitar style (Spratz).

Non-Western Scales, Slides, Calling, Tuning, Movements

Some songs may not be from a western musical background. What can you do?

- Some songs use a different *scale*, as, for example, in some Asian, Middle Eastern and Eastern European music. However, most worship songs from these backgrounds can still be played on western instruments. All that is required is that the tune should be carefully copied.

- In styles that use vocal or instrumental *slides*, it would be good for the musicians, especially the lead vocals and melody instruments, to learn these. In most cases they are not complex. If these features are too challenging, do not let this become a limiting factor. Learn the song in its simpler form and add these details as you learn more. You can be guided by those who know these features.

- In some worship styles it is normal for the lead singer to *call* the next section, speaking it or singing it before the line starts. Many lead singers can incorporate this without much difficulty.

- If a non-western *tuning* is required, you can honour the culture it represents, but rather than dismissing the song out of hand or causing the musicians to feel out of their depth, what about inviting those who know this style to play and sing it as a solo or group offering, or playing a video of the song? It is not necessary to reject a song request simply because the music group cannot replicate this. This is a good opportunity to promote someone else.

- Simple hand *gestures* or physical *movements* may be associated with certain songs and styles. It is good to engage with this. It is worth pointing out that actions and movements can greatly enhance a worship experience since they engage different parts of the brain. Those who feel embarrassed about this should not be compelled to do it, but actions are usually learned quite quickly, provide a very accessible way into the song style and may be a more inclusive approach.

Service Designing

We have focused mainly on songs until now. What about other parts of worship services? Here are certain principles.

Different Languages in a Service

1 Almost every part of the service can include multilingual *elements*.
2 Several parts of the service can be expressed in multicultural *song*.
3 It is good to *explore* various cultural ways of welcoming, greeting, preaching, praying and singing.
4 Almost all multilingual elements require *translation* into the common language (1 Cor. 14.19).
5 Bible readings, prayers and preaching can be led in the *speaker's own language*, provided there is interpretation.

Typical weekly services include various elements, not just worship and the Word. Churches have their own preferred terms for these sections, but there are usually four or five natural and essential sections that create a flow to a meeting and apply to almost every church, denomination, network or church stream. Worship experts tend to group these under these labels: 1) Gathering; 2) Proclamation of the Word; 3) Response to the Word (including Communion or Table); 4) Sending. This 'fourfold order' is recognized by many (for a helpful chart, see Van Opstal, p. 193). We see the beginnings of this pattern in the Gospels, Acts and Epistles and even in the informal meeting that Jesus had with two disciples in Luke 24.13–35 (Cherry, p. 47): 1) Jesus approaches them ('gathering'); 2) Jesus engages them in the scriptures ('word'); 3) Jesus makes himself known through the bread and wine ('table'); 4) Jesus inspires them to go and tell the story ('sending'). In Acts 2, after Pentecost, the church gathered regularly, heard the apostles' teaching, broke bread, engaged in prayer and praise, experienced God's miracles, offered finances and when they went out, they saw God moving in the community (Acts 2.42–47). In the letters, as Andrew Wilson points out, in 1 Corinthians alone worship service elements include the Lord's Supper (chapters 10—11), spiritual gifts and sharing of God's word (12—14), preaching (1, 2, 9, 15), financial offerings (16), a possible creed (15.3–8) and a benediction (16.23; Wilson, p. 123). Relating this to intercultural worship, Sandra Maria Van Opstal suggests that those who design services should:

> *Think through the components of a service. How might you bring in cultural distinctives within the following components: call to worship, greeting, prayers, passing of the peace, Scripture reading, sermon, prayers of the people, offering, Communion, thanksgiving, blessing, and benediction … ? (p. 130)*

We could further extend this to include visual symbolism (physical, digital and video), dress code, preaching and prayer style, the manner of welcome and hospitality and choice of food or refreshments. You could consider which cultures are included in decisions about such matters. At the simplest level, it would not be complicated to invite specific members of the church to bring or suggest what snacks would be appropriate from their cultural context.

Gathering

Before the meeting you can use multiple languages to display a Bible verse or the word 'Welcome' on a screen or bulletin as people enter the meeting space. Then, in the first part of a service, more than one language can be included in:

- A call to worship – a short Bible text or a multilingual song;
- Greetings (with gestures where appropriate);
- Phrases and songs such as 'Praise the Lord', 'Lord have mercy' or 'Christ is risen'.

Proclamation of the Word

Scripture reading can likewise be displayed on paper or screen in more than one language. With the use of mobile phones, listeners can be directed to read along in their language using Bible apps.

CREATING

Preaching will often be in the church's main language but translation can be available in some form. The leader of Mosaic Church in Leeds often brings a copy of his sermon script for anyone whose mother tongue is not English, to help them follow along. Some find ways to provide their script in the language of people they know will be present. Some linguistically gifted preachers may be able to translate themselves, alternating between languages. Realistically, a speaker may feel much freer to express themselves in their own language. It is therefore a common courtesy to offer them this option, with interpretation. This may broaden the range of potential preachers in your church, signalling that language is no barrier to the sharing of God-given gifts. Churches with greater resources can offer translators and headsets.

Response to the Word

Prayer

It can be very stimulating to hear short, spontaneous bursts of prayer and praise in the person's own language. If these are lengthy, it can become tiring and off-putting for those who do not understand. Therefore shorter prayers are best. Prayer for different countries or people groups can use that country's language if there is someone to do this and it can be very impactful, mentally transporting people to that part of the world. If prayers are prepared in advance, translations can be produced.

Statements of Faith (such as Creeds)

Statements that are intended for congregational declaration (like the Apostles Creed) can be proclaimed multilingually, since some exist in multiple languages (Weimar). The words of two languages can be displayed side by side on a screen. If no projection is available, they can be printed or perhaps attractive laminated cards with different languages can be produced for regular use. Creeds can sometimes be sung, including multilingually. For example, a setting of the Apostle's creed ('This I Believe') by Hillsong can be sung in other languages (Songs2Serve, 'Multilingual Songs').

The Offering

You can experiment with different cultural ways of giving money or gifts. This can also be a good moment to include a multicultural song that can be sung and played by the musicians as the offering is being given and collected.

Lord's Supper (Table, Eucharist, Communion)

Phrases like 'Holy, holy, holy' or 'Thank you' can easily be said or sung in several languages. Greeting others as part of the communion service ('passing the peace') could be said between worshippers using their own languages, or perhaps with a suggested simple phrase such as 'The peace of Christ be with you' in more than one language, maybe with a greeting style suitable to those languages.

Sending

Phrases, songs and biblical texts of sending and blessing (benediction) can be done in two languages.

Refreshments/Food

Refreshments, whether drinks, snacks or sharing a meal, provide a relatively easy way to extend hospitality and involve people from various cultures.

Song Choices for Different Parts of Meetings

Multilingual Song Resources and Digital Resources

As mentioned above, resources are available. Those who choose songs will need to become familiar with them if they are to match songs to their place in a service. For multicultural and multilingual songs, I recommend the Songs2Serve website and YouTube channel, with a database of musical materials in a growing number of languages (European, Asian, African, Caribbean). Many of these are especially relevant to churches with diaspora and transnational believers (for example, asylum seekers, refugees and other migrants). As mentioned before, you can find translations of songs by Vineyard, Hillsong, Bethel, Sovereign Grace and others. For themes of Contemporary Christian Music, a growing number of worship websites allow you to search songs by theme. Some of the main multicultural song resource links have been cited before, but it would be helpful to include these again in one place.

Some Digital Song Resources

- Songs2Serve website and YouTube channel.
- Arts Release playlists and YouTube videos.
- Proskuneo Ministries.
- Eric Lige.
- Muyiwa and Riversongz.
- Dan Adler and Heart of the City.
- Taizé.

Songbooks

For hymnbook users there is often additional help in discovering and choosing songs appropriate to different parts of the service or year. Many denominational hymnbooks traditionally group songs under helpful categories. It may not be surprising, then, that several global songbooks use similar headings. For example, the Royal School of Church Music's *In Every Corner Sing: Songs of God's World*, collated by Geoff Weaver, groups 99 songs as follows:

1. Gathering Songs
2. Praise
3. Worship
4. Short Chants and Liturgical Responses
5. Scriptural Songs
6. Psalms and Canticles
7. Offertory Songs
8. Sending Out
9. Justice, Peace and Freedom
10. General

The songs in this hymnbook originate from African Americans, South America, Australasia, Africa, Asia, Eastern Europe, the Middle East and Russia, with singable English translations and performance notes.

Some Multicultural Song Books

- *In Every Corner Sing: Songs of God's world*, compiled by Geoff Weaver.
- *Halle, Halle: We sing the world round*, compiled by C. Michael Hawn.
- *Sound the Bamboo: CCA Hymnal 2000*, edited by Loh I-to.
- *One is the Body: Songs of unity & diversity*, compiled by John L. Bell of the Iona Community.
- *World Praise*, compiled by David Peacock and Geoffrey Weaver, with a thematic index.

The above are just some examples (Ethnic Harvest). Several include supplementary audio and digital resources. Some order songs alphabetically with indexes that may help you spot resources for a section of a meeting. I also recommend that you check the more up-to-date hymnbooks of your denomination or type of church for songs from the global church.

What's Next?

Hopefully, by now you know where to find songs and resources suitable for your church. Perhaps you are using some of these and your church may already have sensed the excitement of seeing God build something new into the fabric of your church's life. Perhaps people from various cultures have met to learn songs from one another, possibly even creating fresh arrangements and translations or composing new intercultural songs together. What is the next step? How can you improve what you have started? That is our next guidepost moving us closer to our destination.

 Questions to Ponder

1. In your worship community, what workshops or other times could be set apart for leaders, musicians and service planners to discover, arrange and create resources for intercultural worship?
2. What existing resources could be helpful for your next stage of the journey into intercultural worship – whether from within or outside your congregation?

9

Rising: Improving and Developing

*Then he said to me, 'Prophesy to the breath; prophesy, son of man, and say to it, "This is what the Sovereign L*ORD *says: come, breath, from the four winds and breathe into these slain, that they may live."' So I prophesied as he commanded me, and breath entered them; they came to life and stood up on their feet – a vast army. (Ezek. 37.9–10)*

First Signs of Hope

Things were happening and Ezekiel had to speak again! And so do we. Previously the bones had 'rattled' and tendons and flesh had been attached. This was the first miracle. But there was no breath of life in them. Ezekiel had to persist in his speaking role. In our situations, the vision may look as if it is starting to come about. We see hopeful signs: some people and materials are coming together. But we still need the whole church to rise on its feet into the fullness of intercultural worship.

Facing Challenges

Typically, challenges can come at this point. As with any change, a small group of enthusiasts or those who feel sidelined wish everything would go further and faster. Others are more resistant. And in between, many think they are getting it or getting there but are not there yet. This could be a rocky moment – but it is not a time to give up. It is quite normal to encounter a collective wobble – a lack of confidence in the whole idea. So far the ground under your feet has seemed firm enough but now some are wondering whether you could easily slip in the mud. This is why we have those ancient guideposts – to keep you on track. As Paul says:

> *Not that I have already obtained all this, or have already arrived at my goal, but I press on to take hold of that for which Christ Jesus took hold of me. (Phil. 3.12)*

Leaders just need to fix their eyes on Jesus, stay steady, set an appropriate pace and keep drawing on God's grace to continue to speak vision into reality. Music and service leaders also need to guide gently, being careful to include everyone in their minds when preparing and speaking – praying regularly for the flock. How do we move on from this in-between state?

Keeping Going

There are important things to prioritize, especially cultivating fellowship by encouraging greater cross-cultural interaction at a social and spiritual level. Unity is the place of blessing (Ps. 133). To that end, it could be beneficial to use some of the tools in this manual, such as the heart-music survey or cultural-preferences grid, as aids to deeper mutual understanding. In Mosaic Church, Leeds, we have seen that taking proactive initiatives has helped significantly. A sermon series on intercultural church, serious conversations about cultural diversity and publicly hearing different voices speaking with honesty from the front has resulted in a greater openness to cross-cultural differences and to building relationships. Worship songs have so far mainly been of a type that worship-band leaders felt comfortable leading but the range of songs has expanded significantly. They include songs that originate from outside the streams we previously drew from. These intentionally represent a more global and international orientation, including songs in various languages. Church members comment positively on the multilingual aspects and the intercultural direction of our church.

Create Inspiring Experiences

Such examples illustrate the need to have inspiring experiences and to prepare these well. Setting the right pace of change in language and music style is also important – to carry as many people together as possible. So how do we create inspiring experiences? It is good to bear three things in mind.

> **When Planning Intercultural Events**
>
> 1 Plan and communicate them well.
> 2 Have fun when celebrating diversity.
> 3 Review them and adjust accordingly.

The same church planned a special service to celebrate 'the nations', the result of extensive discussions by people in a culturally diverse group. The whole service was led by these people and several languages were used, such as in the call to worship and in songs. One person prepared and performed a rap. There was an excellent video talk on multicultural church and a discussion leading into people pairing up to answer a couple of questions to stimulate cross-cultural conversations. The worship space was decorated with flags of all the countries represented. Some came dressed in culture-specific clothing. We had fun, celebrated diversity and gave time afterwards to reflect on this event. From this experience emerged further conversations about intercultural aspects of church life, and there is a sense that using other languages and multicultural songs is no longer strange but something that is part of our church life.

This special service was an inspiring event that elicited very positive feedback. It was designed to experiment with as many ways as possible of expressing 'the nations' among us. Since then, many of these ideas have been fed into regular meetings, some reasonably frequently. That service acted as a catalyst to spark creativity, to break out of the mould and to try things out. Another inspiring experience could be a culture or region-specific style occasion, such as an Asian, African, Caribbean, Celtic, East European or Latin American service. Experiences like these have the advantage of giving people a taste without it immediately changing regular services, but they give ideas that can be incorporated as appropriate. They also provide a way to gauge responses from a range of church members.

Two helpful Attitudes

1 Don't take yourself too seriously!

We are likely to make mistakes in intercultural experiments, simply because we don't understand all the cultures. It's like what people typically learn when working in cross-cultural contexts abroad. We make fools of ourselves with cultural and language mistakes. In fact I often say things in English by mistake, so what chance did I have when learning an Asian language? In Nepal I once intended to ask someone to come back in ten minutes. What actually came out was, 'Please come back in ten years'! The words were not even similar. We had a good laugh. On another occasion I forgot the usual custom of men and women sitting separately in church when I arrived at a large meeting. Seeing a woman our family knew on the right-hand side of the hall, I enthusiastically started heading towards her to offer my greetings before suddenly realizing I was on the wrong side. Whoops!

2 Learn new types of comfort

Most of us are comfortable in our own culture but I was impressed by something a pastor in a church in Minneapolis, Minnesota, told me. He first described how the community around the church had changed in its demographics. Some minority groups had come to church, bringing their cultures with them. The church adapted well to this even if it stretched their levels of cultural comfort. Then he said: 'We have become comfortable being uncomfortable.' This was a striking phrase I have never forgotten. In other words, by embracing cultural discomfort they had learned a *new* type of comfort – they were now perhaps more comfortable in this multicultural reality.

 ## The Result of Inspiring Experiences

If our churches are to move into intercultural worship, people need to think *two* things about it, and both are vital. One without the other will not succeed. If people think it is good but difficult to do, they won't want to repeat it. On the other hand, if it's easy to do but not much good, they still won't want to do it!

'It is Good'

- Vision: 'This is a good way to put vision into practice.'
- Worship: 'The songs help us engage in worship.'
- People: 'Other people will be blessed.'
- Music: 'The style is enjoyable.'
- Words: 'The song lyrics are good.'

'We Can Do It'

- Music: 'Our music group can do this.'
- Words: 'We can sing the words.'
- Adaptable: 'We can make it work for our church.'
- Roles: 'Different people can be involved.'

 ## Beware First Reactions

It is important to note that our first reactions to something may be unreliable as a measure of what is good or do-able. I regularly discover that new songs do not impact me at first. I may feel they are not very good or a challenge to do – but in time I find I embrace them wholeheartedly. The sociologist Gerardo Marti describes this in his book *Worship Across the Racial Divide*. His research shows that people become familiar with new ways of worship over time (Marti, pp. 81–3). It is, then, helpful to give songs time. The risk is that we give up on something too easily. For instance, in one church an Iranian song was considered good to use but when it was introduced non-Iranians were expected to sing too much of the Farsi – making it difficult for the congregation to do. Unfortunately, the song was dropped. It would have been better to review and adjust the amount of Farsi and to try it again a few times.

Review and Improve

Reviewing and improving our creative activities include the following.

Review Questions

- How do the people whose culture is represented feel about it?
- How do other church members feel about it?
- What went well?
- What did not go well?

Improve

Reviewing on the go need not take a long time. Each time you introduce something new, a few minutes' discussion can take place immediately after an event or a few days later. Usually, when a church is exploring a new approach, those involved are willing to make improvements. In the following seven questions we will focus mainly on the use of multicultural songs.

1 Introduction: What might improve how it is presented to the congregation?

I find that it can be less effective if song leaders do not introduce a song well. Good pre-service preparation and clear explanations at the time really help, such as what country the song is from, what language it is in and maybe a brief story or testimony connected to the song. One way to introduce a song is to play it first when people are arriving, moving around in a time of greeting, before or during communion or the offering. This helps people become familiar with it without needing to sing it themselves.

2 Timing: Did it fit well into the service?

New songs are best introduced for all to sing when the congregation is mentally alert. Once people know these songs, the timing of each song is the same as for any song, based on its theme and place in the flow of worship.

3 Language: What will boost confidence and ability to participate?

Before starting the song, some song leaders take a moment to introduce a phrase of the language, demonstrate how the congregation might sing a short section, or show a dance move. This gives everyone a feeling that they can do it.

4 Musical aspects: Were we overambitious or underambitious?

This question is partly for the musicians but also applies to the congregation. For songs with a less predictable rhythm or phrase, the team needs to learn it first. When introducing it to the church, get the musicians to lead that section and allow time for others to join in when they are ready. Two important questions are: a) What parts of the song do the congregation join in with? and b) Are there some phrases that the congregation does not need to sing at all but can be led by musicians or speakers of the language?

5 Participation: How could we involve worshippers more meaningfully?

How much are people from the culture of that song being consulted and involved in singing, reading a scripture verse, praying in their language or sharing why this song is meaningful to them? How is the congregation engaging with the song? Inviting a person (from the song's culture or not) to pray before or after a multicultural song may help worshippers to connect with that song at a different level.

6 Reactions: Are we responding well?

What are people's genuine reactions? Are we hearing the quieter voices? How are we reacting to others' reactions? As we noted above, first reactions can be misleading. What might we do in response to such feedback? For example: a) What do we keep doing? b) What needs a little adjustment? c) What should we defer until a later stage? d) What should we never do again?

7 Expectations: How do we keep building towards acceptance over time?

First, remind one another that the current stage is a step towards a destination. Second, it is likely that people have different mental pictures of what the destination might look like: some may feel your church has already arrived; others may see this phase as a baby step towards something more ambitious. Wise leaders can coach a church through this mix of expectations. Celebration, encouragement and affirmation of each success, however small it appears, are vital means of maintaining a forward momentum and building towards a new future.

Medleys Help Acceptance

Another way to give new songs a chance (or maybe a second chance) to be accepted is to pair songs together: mixing a new song with one that is already well known. Why is this helpful? During the learning process it has the effect of the new being wrapped around by something familiar. Worship-wise it is helpful to find songs where the speed, key and theme are similar. For example, the Hindi bhajan 'Amrit Vani Teri' (Aradhna, 2013) can be paired with the chorus of the song 'Bless the Lord, my Soul' ('10,000 Reasons') by Matt Redman and Jonas Myrin, or with the refrain 'Praise the Father, Praise the Son' (from the song 'King of Kings') by Hillsong.

 ## Projecting Words Helps Participation

People are more likely to accept something new if they can easily follow the words. With multi-language song projection, it is good to get some basics right. There are certain conventions about how to lay out song words on a slide and much of this depends on stylistic preference. Here we consider how to do this for multilingual songs.

Approach

Try for accuracy in language matters but recognize that this usually develops over time. The important thing is to get the church singing a wider diversity of songs and, for literate congregations, seeing the words helps. This need not be complicated. See examples on the Songs2Serve website (such as 'Jalali Yesu' and 'Anta 'Atheemun').

I recommend you get advice from speakers of the song's language. In a smaller church, where people know one another well, there can be a certain tolerance for imperfections, so initially your language advisers may be content with a rough and ready approach in other words, a simpler version. However, over time the accurate public presentation of another language is likely to be scrutinized more closely, especially for those languages where literacy is a high value. For example, make sure you honour these language-speakers by using the right spellings, script forms and phonetic versions. This includes, for instance, Farsi script and its 'Finglish' phonetic version (Songs2Serve, 'Azim Ast Name To Isa'), as well as Chinese characters and the standardized *pinyin* phonetic version (Songs2Serve, 'Wo Di Shen Wo Yao Jing Bai Ni'). Try to use language-appropriate punctuation (like Spanish ¡Exclamation! and ¿Question? marks) as well as accents and markings to show pronunciation and emphasis (Spanish Jesús).[1]

General Layout of Song Slides

1 Simpler backgrounds behind song words are best, so that words are fully visible.

2 Check what colours make words readable both in darkened rooms and when sunlight is shining on the screen.

3 Make sure the font size is large enough to be read from the back.

4 Decide on the positioning of words. Some people advocate setting lyrics in the upper part of the slide, so they can be read above other people's heads. Others prefer a central position.

5 Decide how much text appears on each screen:

- Using fewer lines makes it easy to read but the increased speed of slide changes risks confusion by the person advancing the slides!
- Using more lines allows people see the flow of the song, including the projectionist.
- Using more lines allows two languages to be shown side by side or one under the other.

---

[1] On many computer, tablet or phone keyboards, these can be shown by holding down the letter and selecting the correct option.

Interpretation Helps Understanding

Understanding in Mind and Heart

Another means to improve acceptability and accessibility is to facilitate interpretation. Since almost every part of the service can include multilingual elements, whether sung or spoken, we need to consider the role of interpretation. There are at least two aspects: a) understanding of the mind; b) understanding of the heart.

Mind

In 1 Corinthians 14.19 Paul is extremely clear about the importance of understanding the words: 'in the church I would rather speak five intelligible words to instruct others than ten thousand words in a tongue.' This is why interpretation is highlighted by Paul just before this: 'For this reason the one who speaks in a tongue should pray that they may interpret what they say' (v. 13). And technology can help. Words in the church's main language(s) can be projected, printed, interpreted live by the speaker or translator, and now, increasingly, made available by digital live translation in text form, such as an app on your phone.[2]

Heart

However, there are situations where interpretation is difficult to organize. Other factors play a part and the Holy Spirit himself interprets the meaning of the heart:

> *In the same way, the Spirit helps us in our weakness. We do not know what we ought to pray for, but the Spirit himself intercedes for us through wordless groans. And he who searches our hearts knows the*

---

[2] One church I watched online used Google's Authenticator app for live translation into a range of possible languages. The access code was displayed before the sermon on a screen via a QR code.

> *mind of the Spirit, because the Spirit intercedes for God's people in accordance with the will of God. (Rom. 8.26–27)*

First, not everything in prayer or worship is conveyed by words. Heather, a new missionary in Mexico, was learning Spanish and she felt frustrated in church worship that she could not yet understand all the lyrics. She eventually realized that she could 'worship in a new way' – her heart could worship, despite not understanding all the words in Spanish – not very different from what Paul calls singing or praying 'with the spirit' (1 Cor. 14.15). Although Paul's original application of this was about speaking in tongues, we can apply this to a multilingual context as well: our spirit is praying even if our mind is not.

Second, there are situations where a full translation can hinder deeper understanding. In one multi-ethnic church I visited in 2022, a Ukrainian woman prayed for her country. She had fled from the devastating war in her land. Her prayer was not translated. I don't think there was anyone present who could have translated, but even though we did not understand her words, we could definitely understand her heart's cry because as she prayed she sobbed – her tearful utterances communicated volumes and, in this sense, people could add their 'Amen' (1 Cor. 14.16–17). Reflecting on this, it is possible that a requirement to translate might have inhibited the congregation's heart engagement with her. The important point is that efforts should be made to help everyone understand, but we must admit that human life is multifaceted and going with the flow is sometimes the better option.

Think of the Whole Worship Service

1 The Balance of Diversity in Meetings

In one Friday and Saturday workshop I taught twelve songs from different cultures, with strict guidance to participants not to introduce more than one song at a time in their churches and to make sure that their music group had learned a song well. In other words: 'Please do not overwhelm the congregation with too many new songs all at once!' Later I heard that such was the enthusiasm of workshop participants from one church that they introduced two new multicultural songs the very next day. Generally I would not advise two songs to be introduced in the same service but maybe for this church on that Sunday it worked as a joyous report-back experience.

Over the course of a single worship service, how many songs of other languages and cultures might strike a good balance? In the chapter on heart music, we noted that there is likely to be considerable overlap in musical preferences between people in the church, as well as variety. Therefore it is good for the church to grow into a more diverse musical palette in order to touch more people. By and large, in intercultural worship-music, songs will contain a mix of multicultural songs alongside the church's previously established choices. For example, whatever your normal worship-music style (perhaps liturgical, contemporary, gospel or something else), we could propose four levels of appropriate diversity.

> **Possible Balance of Songs**
>
> 1. Your church's existing music and songs.
> 2. Your church's existing song genres but using other languages.
> 3. Multilingual songs from various cultures.
> 4. Songs of the global church in their original language (with translation).

Churches inevitably bring their own style to the music they do, whether this be classical, cathedral, folk, contemporary, gospel or something else. One example of a gospel-style approach to songs from the global church are the arrangements of an Arabic song and a Greek song by Christopher Mazen in his album *Divine Immigrant* (Mazen). This masterfully illustrates how churches could make songs their own while retaining a feeling of the original song style and, through this fusion, make it accessible to their musicians and congregations.

2 When to Use Culturally New Elements in a Service

I am indebted to Intercultural Ministry Director Jessie Tang for her insight that, in a UK multi-ethnic church, linguistic and musical diversity might more easily be included at certain points in a service than at others.

Opening worship ('gathering')

Mental freshness at the beginning of a meeting can allow for a combination of a familiar song with something multicultural. This can be a good time for learning something new.

Response songs

More familiar songs are probably preferred when responding to a message, especially if the scripture readings, prayers and preaching have been at a deeply personal level. However, familiar songs can include multicultural and multilingual songs already introduced. If response involves prayer for global issues and peoples, songs from relevant parts of the world could be appropriate. Songs for communion are usually songs known to the congregation but might incorporate short sung response phrases in other languages, such as 'Holy, holy, holy' or 'Thank you'. Multilingual mission-response songs could be suitable as a response to a call for action.

Closing songs

The selection of songs for the end of a meeting can go either way, depending on the nature and content of the preceding service. Generally, if there is ongoing personal prayer ministry, quieter, more familiar songs are preferable, but if the atmosphere is robust and celebratory, an upbeat multicultural contribution can be perfect.

 Questions to Ponder

1 What is going well in your church's practice of intercultural worship?
2 What is not going so well?
3 What would help worshippers in your Christian community to say about your intercultural worship experience: 'This is good' and 'We can do it'?
4 What cultural and linguistic mix is most common in your current mix of songs?

10

Integrating: A Culture of Many Cultures

So I prophesied as he commanded me, and breath entered them; they came to life and stood up on their feet – a vast army. (Ezek. 37.10)

By this chapter we have reached the stage where there is a sense that the church is coming alive to intercultural things, 'standing up on their feet'. If you are at this point, it could feel as though your church has found joy in new things, navigated slippery patches, weathered some storms and is coming through to the other side.

Integrating Cultures

'A Culture of Many Cultures'

This evocative phrase of the Malawian mission theologian Harvey Kwiyani depicts an integrated intercultural church (p. 113). He says:

> *The proposition being made here is that congregational life is more whole when in the context of cultural diversity it involves a multicultural community – when people of different cultures commit to worshipping together, each contributing aspects of their cultures to create a culture of many cultures. A truly multicultural congregation will have room for all the cultures within it to thrive, at the same time helping them realize that together they make what the Church is. (p. 113)*

Kwiyani notes that such churches need to balance 'congregational culture' with the 'many subcultures of their members', admitting that 'great multicultural churches ... develop and embrace a culture that makes space for a variety of subcultures to thrive together' (pp. 113–14). He makes the point that overemphasizing individual subcultures can make it difficult for others to engage with them and that in one sense their congregational culture is what helps each to share the gifts of their unique cultures (p. 114).

Let's consider further what this might involve by adding details to the 'Intercultural Integration' diagram in Chapter 4 (Figure 2, p. 41). Integration goes beyond 'welcome' or 'inclusion'. People of different cultures share together on an increasingly equal basis. The key here is 'interaction', shown by the dashed circle. It is where the church, especially the team leading worship, interact across cultures, build friendships, contribute and learn songs and other features of worship.

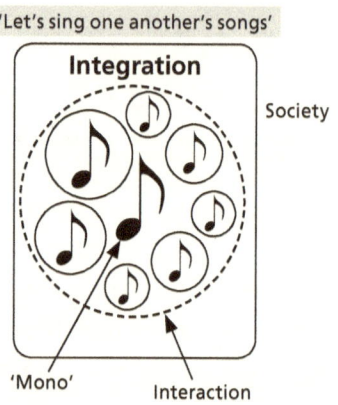

An 'integrated' church may have started as 'intercultural' but most start with one main culture and become more diverse. In either case there are four cultural realities.

1 A 'Kingdom of God' Culture

Christ-centred worship always transcends culture, including the historically common elements that distinguish and unite Christians across the world (LWF, pp. 14–15). This is not to be confused with a particular expression of Christian worship, which is always (consciously or subconsciously) influenced by culture just as the early church was.

2 Societal Culture

Second, each church inhabits a particular society. Its influence is present in most churches – unless the church is culturally isolated. Steven Beck highlights this, describing multi-ethnic churches in Frankfurt as 'mono-multicultural'. 'Mono' refers to German societal culture and language (Beck, pp. 120–37). The early church was culturally diverse but also demonstrated societal realities in its language, meeting spaces, musical styles and cultural illustrations.

3 Congregational Culture (Monocultural moving to Intercultural)

The third aspect is the congregational culture of a specific church – the church's default way of doing things. It covers the main languages and music genres of the church, including its predominant culture(s). It is important to note that congregational worship culture can and does change with time. In some churches, I have seen a shift from monocultural to multicultural, then towards intercultural. Intercultural worship can become the new default, a 'culture of many cultures', the miracle of a new shared worship culture.

4 Diverse Cultures of the People

On the diagram, the music notes represent the worshipful expressions of the cultures in a multi-ethnic church. 'Integration' therefore refers to the intentional mixing of cultures in the team and overall worship culture, resulting in a growing diversity of leadership, languages and music.

Integrating More Cultures

Your church members have probably done well integrating people from your many cultures. Then, just when you become comfortable with this, people from a completely different background turn up and the learning cycle starts again! The previous newcomers now need to welcome the stranger too.

Cultural Power Dynamics

This process shows shifting cultural power dynamics. First, the church's majority culture becomes more open to contributions from their minority culture members. Their warm 'welcome' moves to 'standing with' one another in joys and trials (James 5.13). It requires self-humbling and being willing to receive as well as give. Each culture starts to value the contributions of the others, even feeling: 'We need you.' This is a 'naturally supernatural' process, as leaders submit to the way of the cross in the cultural power differentials involved. Let's examine this.

Gospel Cycle

In the following diagram I have combined the insights of Malcolm Patten and Sandra Maria Van Opstal. First, Patten refers to Eric H. F. Law's insightful 'Gospel Cycle' and Van Opstal cites three attitudes needed: a) 'We welcome you' (hospitality); b) 'We stand with you' (solidarity)'; c) 'We need you' (mutuality). See Figure 6 below (Patten, pp. 80–1; Van Opstal, pp. 62–75).

Patten says that for a multicultural church to continue to develop:

> *the indigenous host community must sacrifice something of what is familiar to them to create the space for those from other ethnic backgrounds to express themselves. Eric Law, a Chinese Episcopal priest,*

highlights the sacrifice necessary in what he describes as the 'cycle of Gospel living in a multicultural community'. (p. 80)

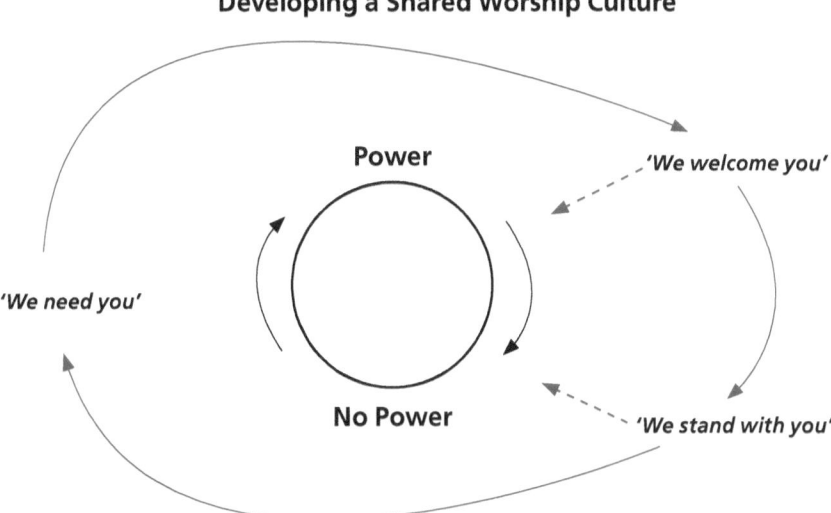

Figure 6

Being willing to 'sacrifice something ... familiar' involves moving from a place of power to yielding up power (the cross) to fresh empowering (resurrection). This becomes a continuous cycle, following the pattern of Christ's crucifixion and exaltation (Phil. 2.4–11) or, as others say, 'The way up is the way down.'

1 Hospitality ('We welcome you')

Initially, people of other cultures are present but the majority hold the cultural power and things are done according to their expectations.

2 Solidarity ('We stand with you')

Then the majority culture engages with these new people, listening deeply – standing with them practically in various challenges. They are expressing the mind of Christ and share their resources. But they still hold the cultural power. The risk is that it stops here. But if they press beyond this, into intercultural inclusion, they realize their privilege and start to lay aside some cultural preferences for the sake of those with less power. They embrace the cross and 'look to the interests of others' (Phil. 2.4).

3 Mutuality ('We need you')

Consciously or not, leaders are sacrificing something of what is familiar. As they do so, they discover that they are being enriched by brothers and sisters from these other cultures. In other words, they sense that they need these fellow worshippers to fill gaps in their own faith and that we complement and benefit one another.

Lifting Others Up

Churches who follow this cycle will be doing what David Anderson describes as 'lifting others up'. He says that this 'includes elevating others and humbling ourselves by allowing others to elevate us' (2007, p. 54). He says that allowing others to give to us and asking them to pray for us is also a way to humble ourselves and lift others up. With such mutual sharing the cycle has completed its first rotation. There will be many more rotations as this cycle transforms us corporately more into the image of Jesus – there is now a more equal sharing of power. Where possible it results in a more inclusive leadership team. This should not threaten the authority of church leaders, unless there is unchecked ambition, pride or prejudice by any party involved. Rather, the decision-making voices about cultural preferences in worship should be expanding – to represent a wider range of people.

Example from Leeds

The above pattern has developed in my own church, Mosaic Church, Leeds. I pay tribute to the leadership, humility and determination that our leaders, notably Matt Hatch and Dan Chadwick, have exhibited to make this happen. As well as listening to diverse voices, they undertook a sermon series for our multisite church in the Autumn of 2020, based on *Gracism* by David Anderson. In one sermon, Matt Hatch spoke about 'lifting others up', referred to above, saying that elevating others is impossible if we keep elevating ourselves. He acknowledged that multicultural worship 'shows our appreciation of other languages in our family' but it also 'humbles the English speakers'. This illustrates the Gospel Cycle, since 'The way up is the way down'.[1] Matt Hatch re-expressed a well-known saying, to which we could add a fourth line for intercultural church communities.

> *Diversity is getting invited to the table.*
> *Inclusion is having a voice at the table.*
> *Belonging is having your voice heard at the table.*
> *Integration is shaping community together.*

---

1 Thanks to Benji Chandra for sharing his personal notes on this sermon.

Developing a Shared Worship Culture

How does this shaping happen?

Mutuality includes:

Mutual Sharing

When you come together, each of you has a hymn, or a word of instruction, a revelation, a tongue or an interpretation. (1 Cor. 14.26a)

Each is given space to contribute to church worship, in song or other ways.

Mutual Learning

Everything must be done so that the church may be built up. (1 Cor. 14.26b)

Each finds they are built up by each other's contributions.

Mutual Valuing

The eye cannot say to the hand, 'I don't need you!' (1 Cor. 12.21a)

Each discovers mutual dependency: we need each other.

Mutual Expression

the whole body ... grows and builds itself up in love, as each part does its work. (Eph. 4.16)

A shared worship culture emerges from the intercultural integration of all contributors playing their part.

To summarize, we can now add these four to our diagram (Figure 7):

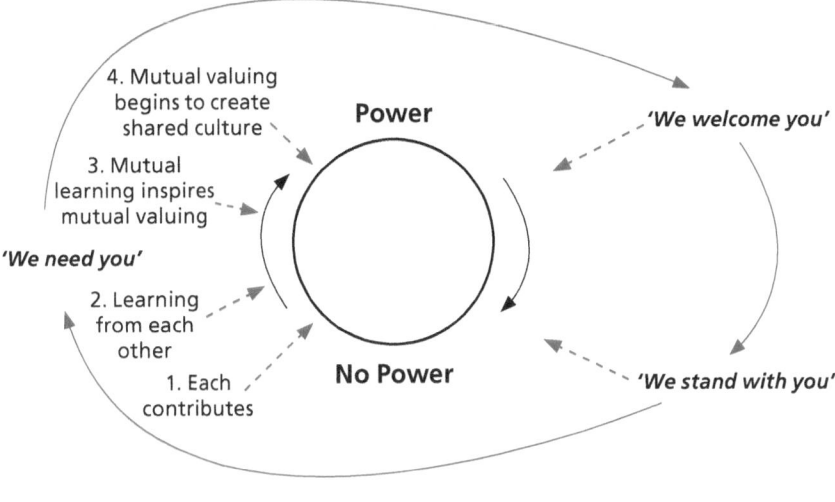

Figure 7

As a church reaches this point, church members feel that these diverse elements are becoming part of 'their' worship. The Holy Spirit is at work. It is a very significant shift, marking that a new paradigm is emerging. Through greater mutuality the church's story starts changing. People start sharing with others their excitement that something like this is happening in their church. Worship times are transformed by what its members bring to church, creating a new culture – a 'culture of many cultures'.

Integrating Intercultural Worship More Broadly

So you've found things that work; a shared worship culture is becoming visible. But one thing remains: to integrate this more fully into the life of the church. Initial experimentations may have become normal but may not be deeply embedded yet. Let's look at this from a broader set of considerations.

AN INTERCULTURAL WORSHIP HANDBOOK

Seven Lenses

Brian Schrag suggests that events be planned around seven areas. Here I interpret what he calls 'Seven Lenses' (pp. 67–86) for a multi-ethnic congregation. I raise these issues now to help with the integration of the principles outlined in this book. These lenses broaden the picture and raise questions about matters that may need some consideration or tweaking.

1 Space: How could your physical worship space be used to express your intercultural breadth? For example, the layout of the room might prioritize cultural styles, such as entertainment (theatre), a front-led, hierarchical approach (lecture hall) or a more egalitarian style (café style). Figure 8 shows a few options but not all. For instance, some cultures honour certain people by giving them seats at the front. Feel free to draw a layout that will help you. Could certain events be laid out differently?

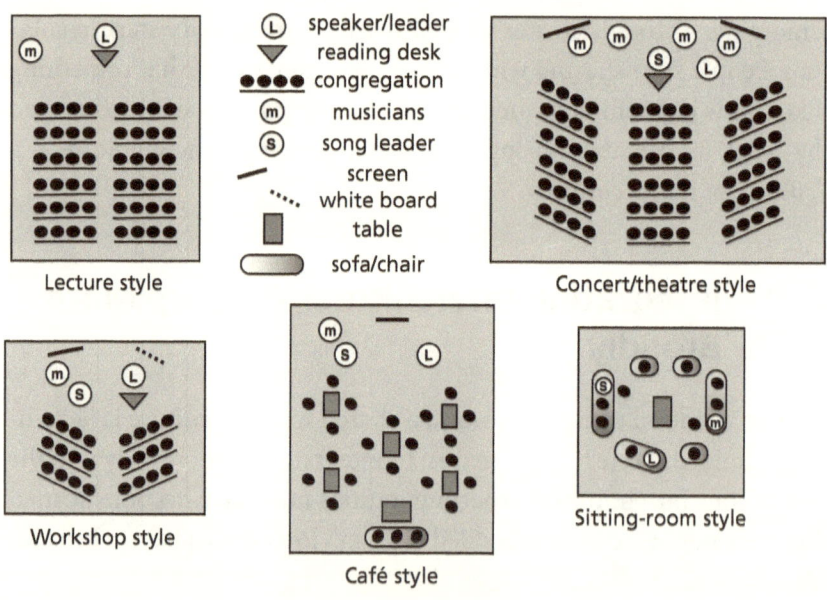

Figure 8

2 Participation: Who could be involved to help you grow into greater cultural diversity? For example, what types of people are invited to lead, speak or sing in meetings? Whose voices are being elevated when discussing diversity? Whose are not? What adjustments would give a better range?

3 Materials: What musical instruments and other objects could be used to express intercultural worship? The music team often decide about instruments but what could add greater musical diversity? For instance, a hand drum (such as a *djembe,* speaking drum, cajon or congas) might enhance your options. What other materials could be significant, such as banners, artwork, flags and maps?

4 Order: What might the shape or outline of a meeting look like to make more cultures feel at home? Christian services share many features but include a variety of cultural expressions. What could be included in your church? What is an ideal length of service? Could you vary the way the offering is taken up or the notices are given? This need not be complicated if it is well explained. It can even be a fun feature but serve a great purpose: to help the church grow in awareness of one another's cultures.

5 Content: What core truths does the church need to convey more often? For example, a church seeking to become warmly multicultural will need to address some key messages in preaching, teaching, prayer and song. What are top topics for your situation and for the different cultural groups represented?

6 Arts: What music and other arts could be used to express your intercultural worship? A cerebral approach emphasizes words and music but typically sidelines other art forms. Intercultural worship can help to engage more people. Some cultures easily dance. Others find poetry meaningful. Many find a picture speaks a thousand words; that calligraphy lifts their spirits. Storytelling (in many forms) is preferred in many cultures. It is good to appraise how accessible our worship practices are for those with various impairments, styles of learning and social engagement. Which arts or digital media will help believers in your congregation engage most effectively? Intercultural diversity often provides resources for a wider range of people.

7 Meanings: What emotional and cultural associations do your music and artistic styles have? What helpful or unhelpful meanings do they convey? What do those involved in designing services need to know to introduce expressions of worship in the most helpful ways?

What Will Your Shared Worship Culture Look Like?

The shared worship culture of an intercultural church will be a unique and fluid mix of their worship culture(s). It will express the transcultural kingdom of God as a local church (within our societal culture), as well as the diverse cultures or subcultures of the worshippers who make up the church. This is what Andy Jolley says about a church's shared worship culture:

> *as well as creating space for each cultural group to express its own distinctive characteristics and to feel valued, it is also vital for a multicultural congregation to develop a shared story and identify what unites them ... Shared new experiences also offer a great opportunity to build a shared history or story that does not belong to a particular group or era. (Jolley, p. 18, quoted in Patten, p. 58)*

Nobody can tell you what this will look or sound like. It will be different because it comes from the *synergy* of your special combination of people. Synergy is 'the combined power of a group of things when they are working together that is greater than the total power achieved by each working separately' (Cambridge). Your new worship culture will be the work of the Holy Spirit among you. However, we can say what, by definition, a new shared worship culture is.

Your Church's New Worship Culture

1. New: It did not exist like this before.
2. Shared: It belongs to this mix of people.
3. Worship: It is your expression of worship.
4. Culture: It is your way of doing things together.

You will describe your worship as 'ours', rather than belonging to one cultural group. You will have experienced the role of the Holy Spirit, 'hovering over the face of the waters' (Gen. 1.2 ESV) of your church, powerfully creating something new.

Preparing the Bride

If you have reached this point, I first want to salute you. Second, I want to hear from you because your story could be invaluable to others. I understand the commitment it takes to pursue this. At various points in church history it has been necessary to restore something that has been lost or sidelined. Today's movement towards intercultural worship is similar. However, we need to resist cultural cosiness. It is a trap caused by the world, the flesh and the devil, where one tribe, race or ethnic group thinks of its own kind at the expense of others. It is a form of cultural pride. But we do not despair. Christ among us is the hope of glory. The worldwide church is more aware than ever, through travel and technology, of its global identity. Many of its international spokespersons are from the global South, so we can rise and stand against such self-centred desires by one culture to preside over others. If we take this seriously, the church can be a countercultural force right across the earth, a shining light and demonstration of how cultures can live, work and worship on equal terms. It is not too grandiose to suggest that the vision of intercultural worship is a call from God to do our bit to prepare the church for Christ's return:

> *I saw the Holy City, the new Jerusalem, coming down out of heaven from God, prepared as a bride beautifully dressed for her husband. (Rev. 21.2)*

This bride, this city, the church, exhibits stunning diversity, a holy people drawn from every nation, people, tribe and language (Rev. 5.9; 7.9). The new heavens and new earth are in some ways 'new' but in other ways there is also continuity with our current existence. Everything is purified (1 Cor. 3.13; Heb. 12.27; 2 Pet. 3.13; Rev. 21.27), renewed or 'made new' (Rev. 21.5), but 'the glory and honour of the nations' will be seen in this city. This seems to mean that it includes the very best of human cultures:

> *The nations will walk by its light, and the kings of the earth will bring their splendour into it … The glory and honour of the nations will be brought into it. Nothing impure will ever enter it. (Rev. 21.24-27)*

The purifying process in some ways starts now! Paul speaks much about what should happen when believers gather to worship as a diverse community. At the same time, he needs to address them about their human divisions, competition (1 Cor. 1.10) and pretensions (2 Cor. 10.5). If he was not put off by what could have been crippling setbacks, we too can take heart. If you are a church or worship leader with a vision for intercultural church, Paul's persistence can provide inspiration.

The River of the Spirit (Ezek. 47.1–12)

Finally, let's remember we are not alone. A truly new shared worship culture cannot be fabricated by human agency. If you allow the Spirit of Christ to grow love and trust between the cultures, it will be a beautiful thing because it is a 'God thing'. At the same time, it will be a 'You thing' – you as a company of Jesus' worshippers. We can go further than this: we will also stop trying to imitate others or a certain worship style. We will still use songs from the historic and international church but will eventually express our unique corporate self as well. We will stop trying to control things and will start desiring something more than our own culture because we see clearly that the worship of Christ is far richer and fuller than any one culture can contain.

As with Ezekiel, the river of intercultural worship starts with God and proceeds to its destination only with his enabling (Ezek. 47.1; Rev. 22.1). At the same time, we need to make a bold decision: to step into the water, not knowing where this will lead. As the river grows in depth, we will need to swim (Ezek. 47.3–5), allowing God to carry us. Then 'where the river flows everything will live' (47.9), including 'healing of the nations' (Rev. 22.2). Despite all we know about human behaviour, the potential of intercultural worship is to heal the nations, because it represents something of 'the powers of the coming age' (Heb. 6.4–5) that even now challenge human and demonic 'powers and principalities'. People of every nation, tribe, race and language will worship God together more freely, equally and unitedly before God. Jesus' prayer, 'Your kingdom come on earth as it is in heaven', is becoming more and more a reality that we experience. And – however incompletely – heaven is being felt on earth.

Appendix A

Seven Top Tips

Seven Priorities

Here, under seven 'top tips', we summarize many of this book's practical advice regarding introducing multicultural elements into church worship. I believe that these seven priorities will apply to many types of official or unofficial worshipping communities.

1 Give Regular Teaching (Chapter 1)

Provide regular biblical teaching that emphasizes the cultural richness of the church of God. It is usually not sufficient to address the topic only once; to keep the vision for intercultural church and worship fresh in worshippers' hearts, it needs to be addressed often, whether as the main topic or as illustrations in talks. There is nothing like recalling the scriptures to reinforce God's perspective. Song leaders can also re-emphasize the vision in short exhortations and biblical references when introducing songs. Apart from Revelation 7.9, other texts might include Genesis 1.26–27; 12.3; Psalms 67; 72.11; Acts 2.11; Ephesians 5.19 and Revelation 21.26–27.

2 Prepare Inspiring Experiences (Chapter 9)

What events could you plan to experience how expressions of diverse cultures enrich worship? It falls mainly on church and music leaders to guide congregation members on this path, so that people say: 'This is good!' and 'We can do it!'

3 Identify Hindrances (Chapters 3 and 5)

What resistance to musical change do you face?

Common Barriers

- A limited or monocultural musical vision for the church.
- Reliance on a limited range of worship 'brands'.
- Fear of the musical unknown.
- Lack of musical skill or flexibility.

To address these, we can promote the following:

- Biblical teaching and positive experiences of intercultural worship.
- Giving time and space for songs from other sources to be enjoyed.
- Learning the most accessible songs first, asking 'What would work well with this group?'
- Holding workshops and jamming sessions, with time to develop skills as musicians.

4 Make it Gradual (Chapter 8)

Introduce things gradually, not in bursts – as with any change. Try the following:

- Introduce easier steps first.
- Explain things carefully.
- Make it do-able, enjoyable, meaningful and worshipful.
- Don't overdo it.
- Repeat it soon.
- Move to the next stage (when ready but don't wait too long).

5 Make it Repeatable

If intercultural worship is to succeed, more than one person needs to be able to lead it, musically and spiritually.

- Have a group learn the song well first.
- Teach pronunciation carefully (but not laboriously).
- Choose people to lead in the 'new' languages.
- Use a manageable amount and mix of languages.
- Use bilingual songs.
- Get enough resources for those leading.
- Encourage and support the learning of musical instruments if you lack people with skills.

6 Keep it Integrated (Chapter 10)

The worship expressions of other cultures will be owned by more people if they are not presented as a performance but are introduced for participation and as part of the entire worship event:

- Introduce new songs with songs people know (maybe as song medleys).
- Do not have only culture-insiders leading the songs (to encourage wider buy-in).
- Encourage the congregation with the benefits of the song, its words and style.

7 Keep the Aim in Mind

The aim is that the congregation values the multicultural elements of worship. They begin to own the vision. We will know this is starting to happen if they speak about it positively to others, if they hum, whistle or sing a song the church is learning or if they actively reach across cultures more. Rejoice in signs of each small movement towards this goal.

Appendix B
Wider Applications

What About My Context?

Applying this to Particular Worship Settings

Every church, congregation or fellowship is different, so you may be thinking: 'I appreciate the need for intercultural worship in medium-sized, multi-ethnic local churches but my context is different. What do I do?' In summary, all or most of the seven priorities listed in Appendix A can apply to most worship settings.

Larger Churches

In large churches there can be expectations of top-quality musicianship, equipment, technical excellence and presentation. These aspirations can create barriers to the introduction of worship materials different from the church's well-trodden style. The music group feels less confident. Leaders may be reluctant to give the platform to people with less background or 'presence' in public. Yet they also know that God loves to use the 'weak'. What can we do?

- We can elevate a diversity of voices in worship without losing standards, including the interview format (with translation if needed) and the invitation to sing or play along with the existing team.
- Language solutions can be found.
- Competent musicians can usually learn skills, with encouragement.
- People can be coached and supported in smaller contexts (such as small groups and language fellowships) as steps to a more public role.

- Larger churches may have resources (people or funds) for musical training.

Multisite Churches

How might intercultural worship work for multisite churches, multi-congregational parishes, circuits, hubs or ministry teams? The key question is: 'How independent is each congregation or site?' If the multisite church uses shared video technology and effectively functions as a single unit, leaders need to consider a single vision for intercultural worship across sites. If each congregation or venue functions more independently, then each worshipping community can develop its own approach, depending on the cultural mix of worshippers. Both models could be developed into intercultural worship.

Multigenerational Church

Generations are cultures. Most of the principles of intercultural worship can be applied to an intergenerational church. Also, each generation within ethnic groups amounts to a culture or subculture, as well as a global youth culture spread digitally across cultures. Conducting heart-music surveys and applying various tools offered in this book could also help to guide multigenerational churches.

A Church with Many Cultures of Different Sizes

Many churches have larger cultural groupings alongside smaller ones. Should the percentages of each be weighted equally in worship? Superficially the answer might appear to be 'yes'. On the other hand, how equal are these cultural groups in terms of cultural power? The Bible teaches us to give preferential treatment to those without power or status (Matt. 25.40). This does not mean that leaders ignore the worship choices of the majority. That could risk marginalizing them.

Rather there should be a fair representation. Each church will need to decide on this question. Likewise it is unrealistic to suggest that many cultural groups can be represented in a single service. It is better to assess worship choices across one or two months. Ask: 'Which cultural groups are being foregrounded? Is there a good spread?'

Multi-Ethnic Small Groups

Small groups of Jesus-followers remind us of the early church's home-based assemblies. As in Colossians 3, people in small groups can bring their own contributions of teaching, encouragement and song. This environment gives individuals freedom to choose songs from their own cultural heritages. For this reason I would suggest that leaders nurture an atmosphere of acceptance of one another's backgrounds, because small groups are a great place for multicultural songs, prayer in members' own languages, cross-cultural sharing of testimonies and biblical insights.

Churches in Monocultural Communities

Despite the cultural diversity of the United Kingdom there are many places that are almost exclusively monocultural. Why do multi-cultural worship in these situations? It is likely that events using approaches advocated here may be occasional, not regular. For these situations, churches recognize that all believers are called to have an outward-looking attitude to the wider world. Multicultural songs and expressions can be introduced, especially for occasions of prayer for countries, people groups, global issues and the persecuted church, as well as prayer for missionaries, missions and people involved in other work abroad. These small steps will also help prepare such churches for a time in the future when other cultures may want to join them.

Diaspora and Ethnic-Minority Churches

The main reason for ethnic-minority or (depending on the country) diaspora churches is to create a home-from-home community where people understand the same language and cultural background. They can be comforted by being culturally understood or not having to struggle with language or discrimination. This suits first-generation immigrants, especially those who have difficulty with the language and customs of the host culture. I identify with this need, since I worked with a minority group in Nepal for several years. They felt that people from their background would resist becoming Christians if they had to join a mainstream Nepali-speaking church; they would have to 'become Nepali' to be a Christian. The differences between the two groups in Nepal were stark enough that the minority group needed to be discipled by people who understood the unique challenges of their background. These are strong reasons for the diaspora or ethnic-minority church. However, we need to admit an intrinsic weakness for the second and third generation, who are usually more integrated into the surrounding culture. They will need a faith community that reflects their culturally complex situation. The solution is often a both/and approach in which they maintain links to their parents' church but where intercultural churches can also play a major part. One example is where diaspora or ethnic-minority churches partner with a church of a different cultural heritage or mix of cultures. One church can 'visit' the other and hold services together as equals. The two churches can grow in intercultural worship, sharing different parts of the service, including leadership and preaching. I have seen a powerful example of this in Leeds.

Churches with Speakers of Non-English British Languages

If your church includes mother-tongue speakers of historic British languages, like Welsh, Gaelic, Irish, Scots and others, the same principles of intercultural worship can be adopted. The Revd Dr Warren

R. Beattie does exactly this. He is a Church of Scotland minister whose congregation, Black Isle East Church of Scotland, includes speakers of Gaelic, Scots and Doric as well as English. On certain occasions, services include Bible readings, liturgical paragraphs and music in English, Scottish languages and sometimes in other European languages relevant to certain members and to the service. In his setting this includes both local and global elements, ancient, traditional and modern, art and folk music, and Scottish psalm singing. He advises leaders of such multi-identity churches to know both 'your context and people', their global and local contexts, to 'curate the music' well and to 'pick your moments' (Beattie, 2020).

Subculture Churches (Youth, Seniors, Celtic, Bikers, Wrestlers and so on!)

Similar questions can be raised for churches designed to appeal to specific age or interest groups. It may be that the evangelistic or discipleship case for a separate subculture approach is strong, as with the minority group in Nepal mentioned above. However, many worshipping communities (churches) like this eventually need to discover how they relate to wider society, including people from a range of racial or cultural backgrounds. Such churches could therefore consider the relevance of intercultural worship and the tools proposed in this book.

Student Groups and Workplace Fellowships

Where students or work colleagues meet for Christian fellowship and worship, they might consider adopting principles of intercultural worship, especially if they are from a range of cultural and language backgrounds. We have seen that a student worship band or a workplace gospel choir might be formed, even just for one event or season. They celebrate their cultural diversity and it is a great way to connect across cultures.

'Our Church has No Musicians'

Several people lament a lack of people to play instruments. There are a few things you can do:

1. When believers gather, Jesus is among you and, fortunately, meeting with him does not depend on music. Make use of the resources and people you already have. The main thing is not to strain to emulate a model of worship that depends on instrumentalists you do not have.
2. Use videos of multicultural songs. See the Songs2Serve website and the YouTube channels of Arts Release and Songs2Serve, among others referred to in this book.
3. Make use of the languages and worship expressions of people in your church community for other parts of the service.
4. Foster intercultural interactions between people. Intercultural church is a worshipping community who love one another.

'Our Church Does Not Want to Go Intercultural'

This book is for those who want to pursue intercultural worship. There are many situations where churches choose not to take this route. However, if there is strong resistance to the idea, it could be for one of two reasons:

1. The *leaders* do not have the vision. Leaders may feel that one culture can best unify everyone. A church whose leaders do not share the vision for intercultural worship should follow the leading of the Holy Spirit and the guidance of the scriptures for shaping worship. God's creativity knows no limits!
2. The *congregation* does not have the vision but the leaders do. Their starting point is probably to establish a vision for church and worship. You could take the church through an examination of biblical, historical and cultural reasons for diversity in worship without making immediate changes. A second step might be to build greater

cross-cultural interaction by hosting social events featuring different cultural groups outside of regular weekly services. A third step might be to gather a roundtable of prayer and discussion between key players to determine the next steps.

Multi-Church Events (Village, Town, Regional or City-wide Gatherings)

When churches in a geographical area plan a joint event, one approach is for culturally diverse churches to each lead a worship time. Others can see, hear and feel their unique worship cultures – a great way to foster cross-cultural appreciation. Alternatively, the same event could provide the opportunity for the formation of an inter-church music team, where a variety of churches lead together. This has the added benefit of relationship building while preparing together.

Worship Songwriters

Songwriters have a special role to play in intercultural worship. What can such songwriters do to facilitate the development of a shared worship culture? First, I would suggest that spending time with people of different cultures, especially fellow worshippers in the same church, could inspire ideas for songs, through hearing their stories. Second, adding a translated chorus to a song they have written could broaden its linguistic appeal. Third, co-creating songs with musical members of the church can broaden stylistic options. How wonderful for a church to have a song they call their own because two or three of their members from diverse cultures have written it together! Established worship songwriters may be reluctant but it may be enriching to co-create with others, each bringing their personal and cultural voice. May the Lord give Holy Spirit creativity in the process, whatever your situation!

References and Resources

Publications (print and digital)

Adeney, Miriam, 2009, *Kingdom Without Borders: The untold story of global Christianity*, InterVarsity Press.
Akhazemea, Daniel, 2015, 'The Reshaping of Religious and Social Landscape of Britain: The influence of the black majority churches', *Transmission*, Bible Society, Spring 2015, pp. 24–6, https://tinyurl.com/bdeys72b (accessed 3.12.24).
Alikin, Valeriy A., 2010, *The Earliest History of the Christian Gathering: Origin, development and content of the Christian gathering in the first to third centuries*, Brill: 211–53, https://www.jstor.org/stable/10.1163/j.ctt1w76wv6 (accessed 3.12.24).
Alzheimer's Association, 2024, *Art and Music*, https://www.alz.org/help-support/caregiving/daily-care/art-music (accessed 3.12.24).
Anderson, David A., 2007, *Gracism: The art of inclusion*, InterVarsity Press.
Anderson, David and Margarita R. Cabellon, 2010, *Multicultural Ministry Handbook: Connecting creatively to a diverse world*, InterVarsity Press.
Avery, Tom, 1996, 'Music of the Heart: The power of indigenous worship in reaching unreached peoples with the gospel', *Missions Frontiers*, Vol. 18, Issue 5, pp. 13–14, https://www.missionfrontiers.org/issue/article/music-of-the-heart (accessed 3.12.24).
Baker, Rob, 2020, personal communication.
Baptists Together, 2018, *Baptists Together Magazine*, Spring 2018, pp. 19-20, https://tinyurl.com/4nk2uphs (accessed 3.12.24).
Barker, Janice, 2007, 'Cosmopolitan Church One Big Happy Family', 'Insight', *Oldham Evening Chronicle*, 22 Mar. 2007, p. 8.
Bartels, K. H., 1974, 'Song, Hymn, Psalm', in *The New International Dictionary of New Testament Theology*, Vol. 3, English Language Edition, Zondervan, pp. 668–73.
Beattie, Warren R. (ed.), 2016, *Ministry Across Cultures: Sharing the Christian faith in Asia*, Regnum Books.
Beattie, Warren R., 2022, *Multicultural Worship*, MA lecture notes for All Nations Christian College.
Beattie, Warren R. and Anne M. Y. Soh (eds), 2022, *Arts Across Cultures: Reimagining the Christian faith in Asia*, Regnum Books.
Beck, Stephen, 2018, *The Mosaik Miracle: How God is building a new church for refugees, immigrants, and nationals*, Greater Europe Mission.
Black, Kathy, 1998, *Worship Across Cultures: A handbook*, Abingdon.
Black, Kathy, 2000, *Culturally-Conscious Worship*, Chalice Press.

REFERENCES AND RESOURCES

Bryan, Steven M., 26 July 2022, '10 Things You Should Know about Cultural Identity', Crossway, https://tinyurl.com/28ms7vxb (accessed 3.12.24).

Calvin Institute of Christian Worship, 16 June 2014, *Nairobi Statement on Worship and Culture Full Text*, https://tinyurl.com/2wbb2xuu (accessed 3.12.24).

Cambridge Advanced Learner's Dictionary, 2024, https://dictionary.cambridge.org/dictionary/english/# (accessed 3.12.24).

Cherry, Constance M., 2010, *The Worship Architect: A blueprint for designing culturally relevant and biblically faithful services*, Baker Academic.

Clifford, Steve, Yemi Adedeji and voices from the One People Commission, 2019, *The [Im]possible Dream: Believing for an integrated, ethnically diverse church*, Evangelical Alliance.

Colley, Ann, 2008, 'Young People's Musical Taste: Relationship with gender and gender-related traits', in APA PsycNet abstract, https://psycnet.apa.org/record/2008-10519-004 (accessed 3.12.24).

Collinge, Ian, 2013, 'Moving from Monocultural to Multicultural Worship', in James Krabill et al. (eds), *Worship and Mission for the Global Church: An ethnodoxology handbook*, William Carey Library, pp. 438–42.

Collinge, Ian, 2022a, 'Intercultural Worship: A contemporary understanding of church and worship in the global age', in Warren R. Beattie (ed.), *Arts Across Cultures: Re-imagining the Christian faith in Asia*, Regnum Books, pp. 119–40.

Collinge, Ian, 2022b, 'Intercultural Worship: Liturgical diversity for the sake of unity, mission and the glory of God', in Elmar Spohn and Eberhard Werner (eds), *Polyphone Klangraüme*, Edition Missiotop, Jahrbuch, pp. 85–99.

Copenhagen, University of, 2022, 'Sociological Study finds Genes play a Significant Role in Shaping our Cultural Tastes', *PhysOrg*, 24 May 2022, https://phys.org/news/2022-05-sociological-genes-significant-role-cultural.html (accessed 3.12.24).

Davies, Madeleine, 2 June 2017, 'Maybe it doesn't sound like it, but it *is* the Church of England', *Church Times*, https://tinyurl.com/yc8r6883 (accessed 3.12.24).

'Davis, Josh and Nikki Lerner, 2015, *Worship Together in Your Church as in Heaven*, Abingdon Press.

Eido Research, 2021, *Mapping Intercultural Mission: Leeds, a collaborative research project*, sponsored by SIM-UK, AWM-Pioneers, OMF, AIM Europe and London City Mission, https://www.eidoresearch.com/reports/mapping-intercultural-mission-leeds?rq=intercultural (accessed 12.4.24).

Fortunato, Frank, Nov. 1999, 'Chris Hale: Bi-lingual, bi-cultural musician from subcontinent', *Global Worship Report*, Vol. 2, Issue 4 (no longer available online).

Fujino, Gary, 2013, 'Japanese Black Gospel Choirs: A counterintuitive approach to contextualization', in James Krabill et al. (eds), *Worship and Mission for the Global Church: An ethnodoxology handbook*, William Carey Library, pp. 274–8.

Graham, Billy, 2015, Billy Graham Evangelistic Association, 19 Aug. 2015, *Answers*, https://billygraham.org/answer/i-dont-like-the-music-at-my-church-should-i-complain/ (accessed 3.12.24).

Gunawardene, Ruwani, 2023, '"Truth Gathering": An intercultural worship journey', *Pioneer Mission Training*, Church Mission Society, https://pioneer.churchmissionsociety.org/2023/12/truth-gathering-intercultural-worship/ (accessed 3.12.24).

Halls, Christopher, 11 Jan. 2019, 'Love for Western Classical Music continues to rise in China', *South China Morning Post*, https://tinyurl.com/yazm8myj (accessed 3.12.24).

169

Harris, Robin, 2000, 'Book Review: Priest, Kersten Bayt. 1998. "Disharmony in the 11:00 a.m. worship hour: A case study of an abandoned interethnic church merger." Master of Arts Thesis, University of South Carolina, Department of Anthropology', *EM News*, Vol. 8, Issue 3, http://ncfmusic.com/media/ext/filebrowser/differingvaluesworship.pdf (accessed 3.12.24).

Harris, Robin P., 2013, 'The Great Misconception: Why music is not a universal language', in James Krabill et al. (eds), *Worship and Mission for the Global Church: An ethnodoxology handbook*, William Carey Library, pp. 82–9.

Hatch, Matt, 2020, 'Mosaic at Home', transcript Sunday 25 Oct. (personal communication).

Hawn, Michael C., 2013, 'Worshipping with the Global Church', in James Krabill et al. (eds), *Worship and Mission for the Global Church: An ethnodoxology handbook*, William Carey Library, pp. 429–31.

Hendriksen, William, 1979, *The Gospel of Mark*, New Testament Commentary, Baker Book House.

Heshmat, Shahram, 2022, '5 Things your Taste in Music reveals about You', *Psychology Today*, 26 Dec. 2022, https://tinyurl.com/483psz4a (accessed 1.3.24).

Hylton, Owen 2009, *Crossing the Divide: A call to embrace diversity*, InterVarsity Press.

James-Griffiths, Paul, 2016, 'The Church Fathers on Musical Instruments', https://tinyurl.com/2f56a77c (accessed 3.12.24).

Jolley, Andy, 2015, *Growing Leaders from Diverse Cultures*, Grove Books.

Kanagaratnam, Anjali, 2020, 'Race, Ministry and Me', *Diocese of Bristol: News*, 20 Oct. 2020, https://www.bristol.anglican.org/news/race-ministry-and-me.php (accessed 3.12.24).

Kemp, Hilary, 2020, personal communication.

Kidjo, Angélique, 2023, 'Born To Do It.' Interview by Alexandra Petropoulos, *Songlines*, Issue 192, Nov. 2023, pp. 30–5.

Kidjo, Angélique, 2024, https://www.kidjo.com/biography (accessed 3.12.24).

Kim, Joy, 2018, 'Diaspora Musicians and Creative Collaboration in a Multicultural Community: A case study in ethnodoxology', Master's thesis, Graduate Institute of Applied Linguistics.

King, Roberta, 2005, 'Variations on a Theme of Appropriate Contextualization: Music lessons from Africa', in Charles Kraft (ed.), *Appropriate Christianity*, William Carey Library, pp. 309–24.

King, Roberta R., 2013, 'Do they have sin?', in James Krabill et al. (eds), *Worship and Mission for the Global Church: An ethnodoxology handbook*, William Carey Library, p. 184.

Krabill, James (gen. ed.), Frank Fortunato, Robin Harris and Brian Schrag (eds), 2013, *Worship and Mission for the Global Church: An ethnodoxology handbook*, William Carey Library.

Kwiyani, Harvey, 2020, *Multicultural Kingdom: Ethnic diversity, mission and the Church*, SCM Press.

Law, Eric H. F., 1993, *The Wolf Shall Dwell with the Lamb*, Chalice Press.

Lerner, Nikki, 2010, 'Multicultural Worship', in David Anderson and Margarita R. Cabellon, *Multicultural Ministry Handbook: Connecting creatively to a diverse world*, InterVarsity Press, pp. 91–104.

Levitin, Daniel, 2006, *This is your Brain on Music: Understanding a human obsession*, Atlantic Books.

REFERENCES AND RESOURCES

Lewendon, Aaron, 2012, 'Worship Music: How should we sing?', https://tinyurl.com/2n-2dan7z (accessed 3.12.24).

Lindsay, Ben, 2019, *We Need to Talk about Race: Understanding the Black experience in White majority churches*, SPCK.

LWF – Lutheran World Federation, 1996, 'Nairobi Statement on Worship and Culture: Contemporary challenges and opportunities', in S. Anita Stauffer (ed.), *Christian Worship: Unity in Cultural Diversity*, LWF, pp. 23–8, https://tinyurl.com/55wvctsc (accessed 3.12.24).

Man, Ron, 2023, *Let us Draw Near: Biblical foundations of worship*, Wipf & Stock Publishers.

Marti, Gerardo, 2012, *Worship Across the Racial Divide: Religious music and the multiracial congregation*, Oxford University Press.

Martin, Ralph P., 1964, *Worship in the Early Church*, Marshall, Morgan & Scott.

Martin, Ralph P., 1978, *Colossians and Philemon*, Revised Edition, New Century Bible, Oliphants.

Mbassi, Constance, 2020, personal communication.

Mbriwa, Sahr, 2019, 'Taking the Narrow Gate: how lament shapes multicultural ministry and discipleship', *Journal of Urban Mission*, Vol. 5, Issue 1, 1 Dec. 2019, https://jofum.com/articles/taking-the-narrow-gate/ (accessed 3.12.24).

McKinnon, James W., 2001, 'Music of the Early Christian Church', in *Grove Music Online*, https://doi.org/10.1093/gmo/9781561592630.article.05705 (accessed 3.12.24).

Merryclough, James, 12 May 2023, '10 Folksy(ish) Eurovision Songs', *TradFolk*, https://tinyurl.com/34f7tftt (accessed 3.12.24).

Meyer, Erin, 2014, *The Culture Map: Decoding how people think, lead, and get things done across cultures*, Public Affairs.

Miller, Terry E. and Andrew Shahriari, 2006, *World Music: A global journey*, Routledge.

Montagu, Jeremy, 2002, *Musical Instruments of the Bible*, Scarecrow Press.

Morris, Leon, 1980, *The First Epistle of Paul to the Corinthians*, Tyndale/Eerdmans.

Page, Christopher, 2016, in Gresham College, *The Music of the First Christians*, https://www.gresham.ac.uk/watch-now/music-first-christians (accessed 3.12.24).

Patten, Malcolm, 2016, *Leading a Multicultural Church*, SPCK.

Piper, John, 1993, *Let the Nations Be Glad: The supremacy of God in missions*, InterVarsity Press.

Piper, John, 1998, 'Every race to reign and worship', 18 Jan. 1998, *desiringGod*, https://tinyurl.com/mwkam7u8 (accessed 9.3.21).

Piper, John, 2016, 'Why Christians love diversity', 31 Mar. 2016, *desiringGod*, https://tinyurl.com/bddye7ak (accessed 3.12.24).

Roach, Jason and Jessamin Birdsall, 2022, *Healing the Divides: How every Christian can advance God's vision of racial unity and justice*, The Good Book Company, e-book.

Roberts, Alice, 2015, *The Celts: Search for a civilization*, Heron Books.

Robertson, Alec, 1960, *The Pelican History of Music, 1: Ancient forms to polyphony*, Penguin Books.

Rogers, Evan, 2006, 'Culture Shock', *Newfrontiers Magazine*, Vol. 2, Issue 13, Jan.–Mar. 2006 (no longer available online).

Russell, Ian, 2021, '"While Shepherds Watched their Flocks by Night:" A paradigm of English village carolling for three centuries', *European Journal of Musicology*, Vol. 21, No. 1, 2021, pp. 81–104.

Saurman, Mary E., 1995, 'The Effect of Music on Blood Pressure and Heart Rate', *EM News*, Vol. 4, Issue 3, pp. 1–2.

Saurman, Todd and Mary-Beth, 2010, personal communication.

Schrag, Brian (author) and James Krabill (ed.), 2013, *Creating Local Arts Together: A manual to help communities reach their kingdom goals*, William Carey Library.

Schrag, Brian, 2025, *Creating Local Arts Together, Revised and Updated: A manual to help communities reach their kingdom goals*, Littleton, CO: William Carey Publishing.

Seevaratnam, Mohan, CCX, Feb. 2021, *Pioneer Stories: Mosaic Church*, interview by Philippa Guy with Mohan Seevaratnam, https://ccx.org.uk/content/mosaic-church/ (accessed 3.12.24).

Sellgren, Katherine, *BBC News*, 6 Aug. 2015, 'Britons "nervous to speak foreign language when abroad"', https://tinyurl.com/372548v5 (accessed 21.2.24).

Silkroad, 'Our Mission', https://www.silkroad.org/ (accessed 3.12.24).

Tang, Jessie, 2018, 'Fieldwork Assignment: Theory and method in ethnomusicology', SOAS, University of London.

Tang, Jessie, 2019, 'BBC Cultural Identity: Exploring music and identity among the second-generation Chinese in Britain', Master's dissertation, SOAS, University of London.

Tang, Jessie, 2020, personal communication.

Tarawalie, Sheka, 2019, *Pope Francis, Politics and the Mabanta Boy: A journalist's journey with God and humanity*, Matador.

Ulebor, Jonah, 2020, personal communication.

United Kingdom Office for National Statistics, 2021, 'Ethnic Group, England and Wales: Census 21', section 2, 'Ethnic groups in England and Wales', https://tinyurl.com/26mm8ajt (accessed 30.12.2024).

United Kingdom Office for National Statistics, 29 Nov. 2022, 'Ethnic Group, England and Wales: Census 2021', section 4, 'How ethnic composition varied across England and Wales', https://tinyurl.com/4es96rr8 (accessed 3.12.24).

Van Opstal, Sandra Maria, 2016, *The Next Worship: Glorifying God in a diverse world*, InterVarsity Press.

Van Velden, Ryk, 5 Oct. 2011, 'Different Models for Multicultural Congregations and Ministries', *Iron shapes iron*, https://tinyurl.com/47ew3yzx (accessed 3.12.24).

Weimar, Harry, 2018, 'The Apostles' Creed in Multiple Languages', *Knowing Jesus Christ*, https://www.knowingjesuschrist.com/the-apostles-creed (accessed 3.12.24).

Wheatley, Judith, 2018, 'Anderson Baptist Church, Reading', *Baptists Together Magazine*, Spring 2018, pp. 19–20, https://tinyurl.com/2azkympn (accessed 3.12.24).

Whitesel, Bob, 2014, 'Five Types of Multicultural Churches: A new paradigm evaluated and differentiated', *Great Commission Research Journal*, Vol. 16, Issue 1, Summer 2014, pp. 22–35, https://place.asburyseminary.edu/gcrj/vol6/iss1/3/ (accessed 3.12.24).

Williams, Kenneth, 2016, *Sharpening Your Interpersonal Skills*, Colorado Springs, CO: International Training Partners.

Wilson, Andrew, 2018, *Spirit and Sacrament: An invitation to eucharistic worship*, Zondervan.

REFERENCES AND RESOURCES

Music Books

Bell, John L. (compiler), 2000, *One is the Body: Songs of unity & diversity*, Wild Goose Publications.

Hawn, C. Michael (compiler), 1999, *Halle, Halle: We sing the world round*, Teacher's Edition, Choristers Guild.

Peacock, David and Geoffrey Weaver (compilers), 1995, *World Praise*, Combined Music Edition, Marshall Pickering.

Loh, I-to (ed.), 2000, *Sound the Bamboo: CCA Hymnal 2000*, Taiwan Presbyterian Church Press.

Weaver, Geoffrey (compiler), 2008, *In Every Corner Sing: Songs of God's World*, The Royal School of Church Music (RSCM).

Audio and Videos

Aradhna, 26 January 2013, *Live in Concert*, https://aradhna.bandcamp.com/track/amrit-vani (accessed 3.12.24).

Aradhna – Topic, 28 January 2015, *Amrit Vani*, https://youtu.be/kqu8rCIRZeg (accessed 3.12.24).

Arts Release Website, Music, no date, https://artsrelease.org/en/resources/playlists (accessed 3.12.24).

Arts Release, 2018, YouTube channel, https://www.youtube.com/c/ArtsRelease (accessed 3.12.24).

Bethelmusic Website, no date, https://license.bethelmusic.com (accessed 3.12.24).

Canaan Hymns, no date, https://artsrelease.org/en/resources/canaan-hymns (accessed 3.12.24).

Cee Jay Music Ministry, 15 January 2020, *Tell am Tenki (Thank you) by Cee Jay*, https://www.youtube.com/watch?v=QcELjeAvhx8 (accessed 3.12.24).

Chrześcijańska muzyka z tekstem, 1 November 2017, *Przyjaciela Mam*, https://youtu.be/GUiwNINfdOg?feature=shared (accessed 3.12.24).

Elam TV, YouTube channel, 2011, https://www.youtube.com/user/ELAMTV (accessed 3.12.24).

Elevation Worship, https://www.elevationworship.com (accessed 3.12.24).

Elevation Worship (for 'Variants of "The Blessing" Song', see below)

Ethnic Harvest, 2015, Resources for Multicultural Ministry, http://www.ethnicharvest.org/links/music.htm (accessed 3.12.24).

Godfrey, Tim, 2020, in Ghits256, 18 April 2020, *Narekelemo Tim Godfrey ft Travis Greene – Nara (Official Video)*, https://www.youtube.com/watch?v=mKlY4O8cwzc (accessed 3.12.24).

Heart of the City Band, YouTube channel, https://www.youtube.com/@HeartoftheCityBand (accessed 3.12.24).

Hillsong, Translations, no date, https://tinyurl.com/5n75hve5 (accessed 3.12.24).

Hilton III, John, 29 July 2021, *The Oxyrhynchus Hymn with English Subtitles*, https://tinyurl.com/3bnspett (accessed 3.12.24).

Hymnary.org, no date, https://hymnary.org/advanced_search (accessed 3.12.24).

Jaago Music, 19 December 2020, *Ek Naam – Jaagoacoustic [official music video 4K]*, https://youtu.be/Nx_m6KP4AJY, Hindi (accessed 3.12.24).
K-Love Staff, 6 October 2020, *Five Versions of Waymaker You Have to Hear*, https://tinyurl.com/mp2z5uf2 (accessed 3.12.24).
Kalameh, Elam Ministries, 2025a, https://www.kalameh.com/en (accessed 3.12.24).
Kalameh, YouTube channel, 2025b, https://tinyurl.com/4jeam8ju (accessed 3.12.24).
Lige, Eric, YouTube channel, https://www.youtube.com/@EricLigeMusic (accessed 3.12.24).
Masihian Music, 18 September 2017, *Mukti Dilaye Yeshu Naam Retromix | Masiahian Music | Hindi Christian Song*, https://tinyurl.com/5469pa3y (accessed 3.12.24).
Mazen, Christopher, *Divine Immigrant*, Bandcamp, 21 February 2022, Anta 'Atheemun (feat. Sarah Lebert and Adora Passos), https://tinyurl.com/4nze9cvu (accessed 3.12.24).
Muyiwa and Riversongz, Officialmuyiwa YouTube channel, Joined 2008, https://www.youtube.com/@Officialmuyiwa (accessed 3.12.24).
Muyiwa, Official, 24 July 2019, *Holy Holy Holy*, https://tinyurl.com/psu3pwth (accessed 3.12.24).
Muyiwa, in Willie Ellebie Gospel channel, 15 May 2020, *Once You Have Spoken* – Muyiwa and Riversongz, https://youtu.be/viVsq0_dVy8 (accessed 3.12.24).
One World Link Warwick, 23 November 2020, *Tel am tenki BDEC NGR*, https://tinyurl.com/525kr7m2 (accessed 3.12.24).
Passion Music, 13 April 2013, *Passion – How Great is Our God*, World Edition, https://tinyurl.com/yujmyz4y (accessed 3.12.24).
Phillips, Rhema, 12 September 2016, *Mukthi Dilaye Yeshu Naam – Lyrics*, https://youtu.be/CoMss9lfHXc (accessed 3.12.24).
Proskuneo Ministries, *One*, https://proskuneo.org/product/one-album/ (accessed 3.12.24).
Proskuneo Ministries, Song Library, https://proskuneo.org/resources/song-library/ (accessed 3.12.24).
Resonance and friends, Arts Release, 7 August 2020, *Nara Ekele Mo (Global Version)*, https://youtu.be/hxSvSmjmCmE (accessed 3.12.24).
SAVAE – San Antonio Vocal Arts Ensemble in NPR, 20 April 2003, *Music from the Time of Jesus: Ensemble Recreates Sacred Songs of Ancient Times*, https://tinyurl.com/mt9rfkun (accessed 3.12.24).
Selah Videos, The, 19 Jan 2022, *Selah – One Name (Ek Naam) [Official Music Video]*, https://youtu.be/RRH4MoA3BkE (English, accessed 3.12.24).
Songs2Serve, Songs, no date, https://songs2serve.eu/songs (accessed 3.12.24).
Songs2Serve, Resources, no date, https://songs2serve.eu/resources (accessed 3.12.24).
Songs2Serve, Multilingual Songs, no date, https://songs2serve.eu/well-known-songs-translated/ (accessed 3.4.2025).
SongSelect by CCLI, 2024, *Songs by Language*, https://songselect.ccli.com/search/language (accessed 3.12.24).
Spratz, George, 2 February 2023, *Highlife Guitar Style: Broken Down*, https://youtu.be/BVVhy3Vz2z0?feature=shared (accessed 3.12.24).
Taizé, Mostar 7 June 2009, *Taizé – Nada te turbe*, https://youtu.be/go1-BoDD7CI?feature=shared (accessed 3.12.24).
Victory Worship, 28 January 2019, *Tribes (Official Music Video)*, https://youtu.be/66H4m-LGgZ54?feature=shared (accessed 3.12.24).
VineyardSongs, Translations, no date, https://vineyardsongs.com/free-christian-worship-songs-translations/ (accessed 3.12.24).

REFERENCES AND RESOURCES

Worship Central South Africa, 26 January 2018, *Come Holy Spirit (Uthando) Lyric Video – LIVE at LIV*, https://www.youtube.com/watch?v=UKAlsYb2V6o (accessed 3.12.24).

Variants of 'The Blessing' Song

1 Elevation Worship, 6 Mar. 2020, 'The Blessing', with Kari Jobe and Cody Carnes, https://youtu.be/Zp6aygmvzM4 (accessed 3.12.24).
2 Destiny Africa Children's Choir, 2 June 2020, 'The Blessing', a capella, https://youtu.be/Gq0LWHX7odM (accessed 3.12.24).
3 Passion City Church, 11 May 2020, 'The Blessing', symphonic version, https://youtu.be/GrBLSBdL8J0 (accessed 3.12.24).
4 Benny Prasad, 28 June 2020, 'The Blessing: A taste of heaven; the Indian way in 31 languages', https://youtu.be/Eb7g7-IIKVc (accessed 3.12.24).
5 Miura Sammy, 1 Aug. 2020, 'The Blessing', Japanese, https://youtu.be/qNEQnC8piWA (accessed 3.12.24).
6 The Greater Middle East Blessing, 3 Sept. 2020, 'The Lord's Prayer and the Blessing', https://youtu.be/VJSQNDQI0bs (accessed 3.12.24).

Contacts

Ian Collinge: interculturalworship@gmail.com
All Nations Christian College, https://www.allnations.ac.uk

Arts Release and Resonance Bands[1]

Arts Release, https://artsrelease.org
Arts Release YouTube, https://www.youtube.com/@ArtsRelease
Arts Release Facebook, loveartsrelease
Arts Release Music, https://artsrelease.org/en/music-worship
Arts Release Email, artsrelease.admin@wec-uk.org
Resonance Band, resonancebands.org

---

1 The global Resonance multicultural worship collective is currently made up of three bands, mostly functioning regionally and occasionally combining, digitally, as one.

www.ingramcontent.com/pod-product-compliance
Lightning Source LLC
Chambersburg PA
CBHW022221090526
44585CB00013BB/664